# SNAZAROO ZOO

## GReat FacEs aNd Easy CoStumes to BRing Out the Animal in You

**JANIS BULLIS**

**krause publications**

700 E. State Street • Iola, WI 54990-0001

P9-BYL-516

Copyright © 1997 by Janis Bullis

All Rights Reserved

Published by

**krause publications**

700 E. State Street • Iola, WI 54990-0001
Telephone: 715/445-2214

Please call or write for our free catalog of publications.
Our toll-free number to place an order or obtain a free
catalog is 800-258-0929 or please use our regular busi-
ness telephone 715-445-2214 for editorial comment and
further information.

Designed by Anthony Jacobson
Photography by Donna Chiarelli
Illustrations by Joy Powell

Manufactured in the United States of America
Library of Congress Cataloging-in-Publication Data

Bullis, Janis.
    Snazaroo zoo : great faces and easy costumes to bring out the
animal in you / Janis Bullis.
        p.        cm.
    ISBN 0-8019-8940-X
    1. Face painting.  2. Costume.  I. Title.
TT911.B85     1997
745.5—dc21                                    96-38024
                                                    CIP

1 2 3 4 5 6 7 8 9 0      6 5 4 3 2 1 0 9 8 7

# ACKNOWLEDGMENTS

A very special thank you to:

✱ Kunin Felt Company Inc., a Foss Manufacturing Company, for
providing felt fabric in just the right colors and textures.

✱ Prym-Dritz Corporation, not only for the sewing notions, but
also for their "My Double" dress form. It proved to be indis-
pensable when all the pint-sized models were fast asleep.

✱ Freudenberg Nonwovens, Pellon Division, for the Wonder
Under fusible web, which always adds a professional touch.

✱ Black and Decker, Inc., for their 2-Temp glue gun and gener-
ous supply of glue.

✱ Snazaroo, for their terrific paints, brushes, and expertise.

✱ Ashley Anderson, Kayla Decker, and Clarke Mayer, for standing patiently in the costume prototypes while I stitched,
pinned, and trimmed.

✱ Natalie Cox, Nicole Lynn Craig, Brooke Donegan, Jessica
Holmes, Stephanie Holmes, Cecilia Jones, Kelley Moore,
Lauren Moore, Carl A. Norman, James H. Spearman, Joshua
Taylor, Zachary Taylor, and Cameron Vozzella—all the terrific
children who were thrilled to model costumes that covered
them from head to toe during those long, hot days of photography.

✱ Gary Cole, Lance Peterson, and Darrin Peterson, for so expert-
ly using Snazaroo paints to transform the angelic face of an
8-year-old into a scary, hairy beast.

✱ Cecelia Bayruns and Sean MacNeal, for faithfully transcribing
the painting steps.

✱ My mom, for always finding the time to make my costume,
so many years ago.

Welcome to *Snazaroo Zoo*, where bringing your favorite animals to life is as easy as 1-2-3! All you need is some Snazaroo face paint and a few basic costume supplies. The rest is here: easy-to-follow instructions, color photos, illustrations, patterns— everything you need to start creating wild and wonderful creatures on your own.

*Snazaroo Zoo* animals are so fun and easy to make, kids won't be able to resist helping out. Each animal is based on a one-color costume body that can be sewn or purchased (a sweat suit works fine if you don't have the time to sew). Then, unique "accessories"—wings made of cardboard, a turtle shell created from a garbage can lid, a stuffed tail, or extra legs—are attached using the easy, step-by-step instructions. In most cases, a few hand stitches and some fabric glue are all that's needed.

The animal's ears or antennae add a lifelike touch. Attach them to a sewn hood that matches the costume or to a ribbon-covered headband. You choose the technique you like best based on the look you want and the time you can spend (headbands require no sewing).

These animals have a timeless quality. Of course, dressing up like a beautiful butterfly or a scary spider will always have appeal, but what makes these animals last is their ability to change into one another, as if by magic. Once the basic costume body is made, some scissors, glue, and cardboard can change a lady bug into a chimpanzee in no time. The basic black costume alone can be changed into 8 different animals. Simply remove the wings and add a tail, or make another easy change. This means big sister's green turtle costume can be handed down to little brother several years later. He can simply remove the turtle shell and stitch on an armor-plated tail to become his favorite green dinosaur.

But none of these animals would be complete without a colorful painted face. You can create the perfect twitching nose, some scary fangs, or a first-rate set of whiskers by following the step-by-step photographs for each animal. Snazaroo water-based face paint (available at most craft stores) makes the task oh-so-easy and even more fun. Simply apply the Snazaroo paint with brushes and sponges. If you make a mistake, soap and warm water or a moistened towelette will let you "erase" and start again!

So flip through the five "exhibits" in this zoo, choose your favorite animals, and get ready to have fun! Don't miss the special boxes that tell you how to act like each animal. And, before you start assembling your first costume or painting your first face, be sure to review the General Instructions on pages 72 to 83. Above all, relax and have a good time—this zoo is only as wild or as tame as you make it!

LOVABLE PETS

# CURIOUS CAT

## How to Paint the Face

**1.** Using a damp sponge and Barely Beige #909, cover the upper eye area (including the eyelids and eyebrows), upper lip area, and chin.

**2.** Using a damp sponge and Ochre Yellow #244, cover the forehead, nose, and apples of cheeks.

**3.** Using a damp sponge and Rust Brown #977, cover the upper forehead, cheeks, and jawbone. Using a clean sponge, blend the rust brown into the ochre yellow on the forehead and cheeks.

**4.** Using a medium flat brush and Black #111, create a "snout" by drawing zigzag lines from the outer nostrils to the corners of the mouth and then down under the chin. Paint the tip of the nose and draw a line connecting it with the center of the upper lip. Paint a zigzag circle around each eye, starting above the eyebrow and continuing down across the top of the cheek. Then, add a curved line from the start of the zigzag above the eyebrow down between the nose and the eye. Draw short, horizontal lines across the bridge of the nose. Paint the lips and add "whisker dots" to the "snout" and whiskers to the cheeks.

Finally, add a touch of black just below the hairline, on both sides of the forehead.

## YOU WILL NEED

* sweat suit or sewn costume body
* ribbon-covered headband or sewn hood
* ⅜ yd. of 36"-wide cinnamon felt for ears and tail
* ⅜ yd. of 36"-wide charcoal felt for ears and chest
* polyester stuffing
* black gloves
* black bumpy chenille stems

## How to Make the Costume

Because cats come in many colors, you can choose from a wide variety of felt and sweat suit colors. Cat ears can be easily attached to a hood or a headband, whichever the child prefers.

**1.** Purchase a sweat suit or sew a costume body. Also make a ribbon-covered headband or sew a felt hood. (See General Instructions.)

**2.** To make the Long Tail pattern, draw a 5" × 31" rectangle on paper. Using the Cat Ear and Cat Chest patterns on page 85, transfer the patterns onto paper (see General Instructions).

**3.** Using the paper patterns, cut 1 tail piece and 4 ear pieces from cinnamon felt. Cut 2 ear pieces and 1 chest piece from charcoal felt. Trim 1" from 2 outer curves of charcoal felt ears to create ear insets.

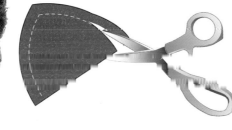

**4.** While the child is wearing the sweatshirt or costume, carefully pin on the chest piece with the wider part at the bottom. Remove the shirt or costume and stitch or glue the chest piece to the costume front.

**5.** For each ear, stitch or glue 2 cinnamon-felt ear pieces together for added weight and body. Glue 1 ear inset to each ear front, keeping the bottom edges even. Weigh down the ears with some heavy books until they are dry.

**6.** To apply the ears to the hood or headband, pin them at an equal distance from the center of the hood or band, then glue or stitch them on, leaving 1 to 2 inches of space between the ears.

**7.** With the right sides facing, fold the tail piece in half lengthwise. Pin and stitch a seam along the long edge and 1 short end. Trim the seam allowance to ¼".

**8.** To simplify the stuffing process, turn the tail to the right side and stuff it at the same time. Begin by using the eraser end of a pencil to poke in the stitched end a few inches. Insert stuffing into those few inches. Push a few more inches of the tail and add more stuffing. Continue until the entire tail is turned and stuffed.

**9.** Position the tail below the zipper on the costume or on the seat of the sweatpants. Adjust the length as needed by trimming from the open end. Using long hand stitches, attach the open end of the tail to the costume, with the stitched long edge facing down toward the body.

**10.** To make the claws, cut apart 5 sections of bumpy chenille, making a cut at each thin connecting segment. Next, cut each section in half to yield 10 claws. Stitch the widest part of each half to a glove finger tip. (Every finger should have 1 claw.) To soften the tips and avoid dangerous scratches, fold under ¼" of the wired end on each claw.

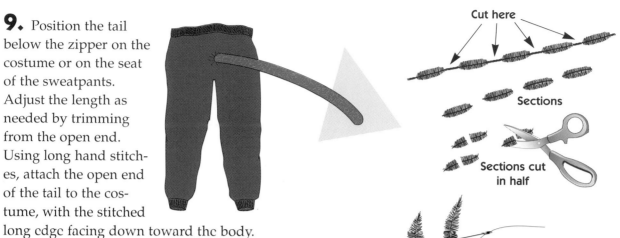

Cut here

Sections

Sections cut
in half

## HOW TO ACT LIKE A CURIOUS CAT

✱ To imitate a cat, kneel on the ground on all fours and arch your back; now wag your tail slowly and make a purring sound. Walk very quietly and extend your claws to climb.

✱ Can you curl your tongue? This is what cats must do to drink. Make a small cup shape with your tongue to pretend that you're lapping up some water or milk.

✱ Cats can run faster and hear better than dogs. Practice running fast on all fours and listening carefully to the sounds around you.

✱ Cats are superb at staring at objects without blinking. Pick an object across the room and stare at it. How long can you stare without blinking?

# TOO-SHY TURTLE

## How to Paint the Face

**1.** Using a damp sponge and Sparkle Green #44, cover the entire face, except for the eyelids and the lower eye area.

**2.** Using a medium flat brush and Metallic Gold #777, cover the eyelids and the lower eye area. Paint 1 arch through the eyebrow, 1 above the eyebrow, and 1 upside down below the eye area. Then, paint 1 line curving out from the center of the upper lip to the middle of the left cheek and 1 line curving out to the middle of the right cheek. Paint the lips as well.

**3.** Using a medium flat brush and Metallic Gold #777, create "turtle spots" on the outer cheeks, down the jawbone, and onto the chin.

**4.** Using a thin-tip brush and Dark Green #455, outline the turtle's "mouth," the eyes and the 3 arches around them, and the turtle spots. Finally, add a few dark green turtle spots for contrast.

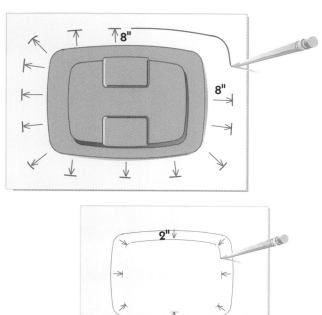

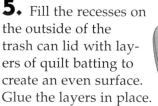

## How to Make the Costume

The turtle's shell is made from an oval or rectangular plastic trash can lid covered with felt and worn like a backpack. (Ideally, the lid should extend from the child's shoulder to his or her hip.) Felt-covered poster board is hung from straps for the shell front. Because the lid is kept intact, it can again be used to cover trash once the party is over.

**1.** Purchase a sweat suit or sew a costume body. Also sew a felt hood. (See General Instructions.)

**2.** For the Shell Facing pattern, trace the trash can lid onto a piece of paper, then cut the pattern out along the lines. For the Shell Back pattern, trace the lid onto another piece of paper, adding 8" to all edges, then cut the pattern out along the outside lines. For the Shell Front pattern, trace the lid onto a third piece of paper, subtracting 2" from all edges, then cut the pattern out along the inside lines.

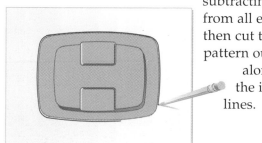

**3.** Cut out a piece of poster board and a matching piece of green felt using the Shell Facing pattern; glue the poster board and the felt together. Then, cut out a piece of poster board and a matching piece of gold felt using the Shell Front pattern; glue the poster board and the felt together. Set the felt facing and the felt front aside for use later. Finally, cut out a piece of green felt using the Shell Back pattern.

**4.** On the side walls, along the short edges of the trash can lid, mark the center of the walls as shown. At one center marking, use the craft knife to cut a slit in the plastic parallel to and ½" from the bottom edge of the lid. At the other center marking, cut 2 more slits, each 3" from the center mark. Each of the 3 slit openings should measure 1½" × ½".

**5.** Fill the recesses on the outside of the trash can lid with layers of quilt batting to create an even surface. Glue the layers in place.

**6.** Turn the lid upside down. Using the Shell Facing pattern, cut enough batting layers to fill the inside of the lid. Glue the layers in place.

**7.** Take the felt back you cut out in step 3 and stitch a row of long hand-basting stitches around its perimeter, ½" from the edge. Leave the thread tails long. Place the trash can lid upside down and centered on the felt back. Gently pull the tail ends of the basting stitches to gather the felt and wrap it around the lid. Tie the thread tails to hold the felt in place. For added security, stitch a spider web of threads stretching randomly across opposite edges of the lid to help hold the felt taught.

**8.** Poke at the felt with your fingernail to feel the slits in the side walls of the lid. Cut identical slits in the felt along those side walls and cut slits "above" those slits in the felt that now extends from the side walls on the underside of the lid. Fold the webbing in half and thread the folded end over and in through the side wall with the single slit. Secure the webbing to the lid by stitching or safety pinning the webbing to itself. Separate the webbing tails and thread them through the slits in the felt at bottom of the lid out the side wall, one tail per slit.

**9.** Glue the felt facing from step 3 to the bottom of the lid to hide the spider web stitches and give the shell a clean finish. If needed, cut notches in the facing so that it fits around the webbing on the bottom of the lid.

**10.** Have the child try on the lid as though it were a backpack. Adjust the straps to fit and stitch or safety pin the webbing to itself to secure it. Do not trim the long tail ends of the webbing. Set shell aside.

**11.** Use the Shell Front pattern from step 2 as a guide in making the green blocks on the front of the shell. Trace the pattern onto a fresh piece of paper. Using a pencil, draw the same shape (a squared or oval circle) inside the pattern, approximately half the size of the pattern. Draw 4 lines across the large circle as if it were a pizza pie, intersecting at the center and dividing it into 8 pieces.

**12.** Change to a colored pencil for contrast. Measuring about ½" from all edges of the center circle, draw the center block of the shell. Measuring about ½" from the outer sections of the pie, draw each of the outer blocks of the shell. To make the blocks look natural, do *not*

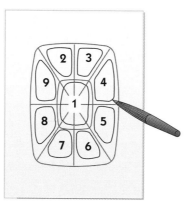

measure accurately: Draw somewhat wavy lines, and round off the corners as you draw. Label the center block 1, then beginning at the upper left block and moving clockwise, number each of the outer blocks from 2 to 9.

**13.** Cut each of the blocks from paper along the colored lines; ignore the pencil lines. Using the paper blocks as patterns, cut each of the blocks from green felt. Beginning with the center block and continuing in numerical order, glue the green blocks to the gold felt front cut in step 3. Set aside. Refer to the photo on page 7 for placement.

**14.** Begin again with step 11, but this time use the Shell Facing pattern from step 2. Continue with steps 12 and 13 to make block patterns and cut and glue gold felt blocks to the back of the green turtle shell. When dressing, put the "backpack" shell on first, then stitch or safety pin the front shell to the tail ends of the webbing.

## HOW TO ACT LIKE A TOO-SHY TURTLE

* A turtle's shell serves many purposes: It shelters the turtle from the weather, it hides him from his enemies, and it protects his or her body from rough rocks and branches on the forest floor. To hide in your shell, squat close to the floor, pull your arms close to your sides, and hike your shoulders up next to your ears.
* Most turtles think leaves, worms, and insects make delicious food. Because these things are not good for people to eat, only pretend that you like eating the things that turtles do.

# DARLING DALMATION

## How to Paint the Face

**1.** Using a damp sponge and White #000, cover the entire face, except for 1 eye (including the eyelid and lower eye area).

**2.** Using a large flat brush and Black #111, cover the unpainted eye. Now, using a thin tip brush, add 2 or 3 dalmatian spots to the face. Paint the entire upper lip and half of the lower lip, leaving space for a tongue. Paint the tip and lower sides of the nose; however, do not paint the nostrils entirely. Connect the middle of the nose and the upper lip.

**3.** Using a thin tip brush and Black #111, draw an arch over the eyebrows. Create a dog "snout" by painting curved lines that extend from the outer nostrils around to the upper corners of mouth. Add "whisker dots" inside the snout area. The lower snout lines should begin from the lower lip and meet at the lower edge of the chin.

**4.** Using a thin-tip brush and Bright Red #0055, create the tongue by painting the unpainted bottom lip and half of the chin. Finally, using a thin-tip brush and Black #111, outline the tongue and draw a short line down the center for dimension.

## How to Make the Costume

It's easy to make dalmatian spots by stitching or gluing felt circles and ovals to the costume body. Although it takes a few minutes longer than gluing, stitching is recommended for sweat suit bodies if you want to return the suit to normal wear once the child is finished with the costume, because stitched-on spots are easier to remove.

**1.** Purchase a sweat suit or sew a costume body. Also make a ribbon-covered headband or sew a hood. (See General Instructions.)

**2.** To make the Long Tail pattern, draw a 5" × 31" rectangle on paper. Using the Dog Ear pattern on page 85, transfer the pattern onto paper (see General Instructions).

**3.** Using the paper patterns, cut 1 tail piece from white felt and 4 ear pieces from black felt. Also from black felt, cut several circles and ovals in many different sizes for the dalmatian spots.

**4.** For each ear, stitch or glue 2 felt ear pieces together for added weight and body. Weigh down the ears with some heavy books until they are dry.

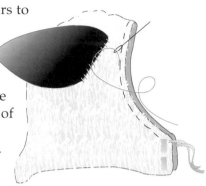

**5.** To apply the ears to the hood, place each ear horizontally on each side of the hood (at an equal distance from the center top of the hood) with the long curved edge at the top and the short straight edge at a slight downward angle. Then, glue or stitch the straight edge to the hood.

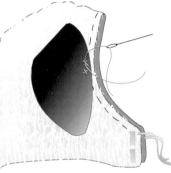

**6.** Fold each ear forward and attach the front edge of the ear to the front edge of the hood, using small hand stitches or a few drops of glue.

**7.** To make the tail, see steps 7 through 9 of the Curious Cat on pages 3–4.

**8.** Stitch or glue the felt dalmatian spots from step 3 to the sweat suit or costume body, hood, tail, and sneakers.

# HOW TO ACT LIKE A DARLING DALMATIAN

* Scientists believe that dogs are ancestors of wolves. They sometimes howl like wolves at the sound of fire sirens and pretend that they are sleeping in caves when they hide under coffee tables. Lie still under your favorite table, then practice your howling sounds.

* In general, dogs are very friendly. Wave your paw at passers-by to show how friendly you are.

* Usually, dogs like to stay close to home and often pick one family member to be their favorite. Do you have a favorite person in your family, or is it too difficult to pick just one? Let your favorites know how special they are by doing nice things for them.

* Just like people, dogs come in many shapes, sizes, and colors. Name all the different types of dogs you can think of and their distinguishing characteristics.

JUNGLE BEASTS

# CHATTERING CHIMP

## How to Paint the Face

**1.** Using a damp sponge and Light Brown #988, circle and color in each eye area starting at the bridge of the nose, continuing down around the eye, across the upper cheek, through the temple, up above the eyebrow into the forehead, and down the bridge of the nose. Then, circle and color in the mouth area, starting from both outer nostrils, continuing down around the mouth and under the chin. Finally, cover the nose and nostrils.

**2.** Using a damp sponge and Black #111, cover the unpainted areas of the forehead, temples, cheeks, and jawbone. Do not blend the black into the areas of Light Brown #988.

**3.** Using a medium round brush and Beige Brown #911, create thick "monkey eyebrows" above the child's eyebrows. Paint the eyelids, the under-eye area, and the lips. Add "wrinkles" beneath the eyes and across the nose. Add "laugh lines" around the mouth and highlight the tip of the nose and the nostrils.

**4.** Using a medium round brush and Black #111, draw a line along 1 side of each "wrinkle," creating a shadow effect. Outline the tip of the nose, the nostrils, and the eyes near the eyelashes. Draw eyebrows above and below the eyebrows created in step 3. Finally, overlap the Light Brown #988 with the black by adding tiny slash marks to give the face a furry look.

## YOU WILL NEED

* sweat suit or sewn costume body
* ribbon-covered headband or sewn hood
* ½ yd. of 36"-wide beige felt for ears, hands, and feet
* 1 piece of 9" × 12" poster board
* 20 false nails
* black or beige gloves
* black paint
* black felt-tip pen

## How to Make the Costume

If a headband is used instead of a hood, be sure that the child wears it in front of his own ears to best show off the chimp's ears. If available, substitute 2 pairs of beige gloves for the felt hands and feet, then glue the painted nails directly onto the gloves.

**1.** Purchase a sweat suit or sew a costume body. Also make a ribbon-covered headband or sew a hood. (See General Instructions.)

**2.** Using the Chimp Ear pattern on page 85, transfer the pattern onto paper (see General Instructions). For hands and feet, trace onto paper the child's hand and arm, measuring approximately 4" up from the wrist.

**3.** Using the paper patterns, cut 4 ear pieces and 4 hand pieces from beige felt. Cut 2 ear pieces from poster board. Trim ½" from the slightly curved edge of the poster board ears.

**4.** For each ear, apply glue to both sides of a poster board ear. Then, position 1 felt ear piece on each side, making sure that the wavy edge of the felt is even with the wavy edge of the poster board. Weigh down the ears with some heavy books until they are dry.

**5.** Using a felt-tip pen, draw several curved contour lines on the felt ears. (Remember, the left and right ears should be mirror images of each other.)

**6.** Separate each ear front from its back at the seam allowances, along the slightly curved, unglued edge where the felt extended beyond the poster board. Then, pin the seam allowances to the side of the hood (in front of the child's ear) or headband, and hand stitch or glue it in place.

**7.** To camouflage the beige seam allowances on the hood or headband, cut a ½" wide strip of black felt or ribbon long enough to cover the allowances, then secure it with glue.

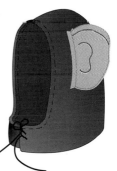

**8.** Paint the false nails black and glue them to the fingers of the felt hands and feet. Once the child has the costume on, tuck the arm extensions of the hands and feet in under the costume cuffs.

## HOW TO ACT LIKE A CHATTERING CHIMPANZEE

✳ Beat your chest with your fists and make growling, blowing, and snorting sounds. Chimpanzees do this when they are happy, frightened, or angry.

✳ When you walk, rock back and forth from leg to leg and swing your arms. Roll your shoulders forward and try to make your knuckles touch the ground.

✳ Baby chimps like to run, jump, climb, and spin. Do any or all of these things to show what a playful chimp you are!

# FEROCIOUS LION

## How to Paint the Face

**1.** Using a damp sponge and White #000, cover the eyelids, eyebrows, upper lip area, and chin.

**2.** Using a damp sponge and Light Beige #910, cover the temples, forehead, nose, cheeks, and jawbone.

**3.** Using a damp sponge and Beige Brown #911, add contrast to the temples, cheekbones, and sides of the face and underneath the chin. Blend the beige brown areas into the Light Beige #910 areas.

**4.** Using a medium flat brush and Black #111, create a "furry snout" by drawing zigzag lines from the outer nostrils to the corners of the mouth. Also, outline the White #000 on the chin and upper eyes with zigzag lines. Paint the tip of the nose, nostrils, and lips black. Paint a line from the tip of the nose to the center of the upper lip. Finally, add "whiskers" to the cheeks and "whisker dots" to the upper lip.

**YOU WILL NEED**

* sweat suit or sewn costume body
* sewn hood
* 3/8 yd. of 36"-wide beige felt for ears and tail
* 1/2 yd. of 36"-wide rust fur for collar and tail tuft
* polyester stuffing
* beige gloves
* beige bumpy chenille stems

## How to Make the Costume

A combination of plush felt and fake fur is perfect for this costume. Once completed, the fur hood and collar will appear as a one-piece mane; however, the materials and the assembly instructions for each are separate. Headband-mounted ears are not recommended for this costume.

**1.** Purchase a sweat suit or sew a costume body. Also sew a felt hood. (See General Instructions.)

**2.** To make the Long Tail pattern, draw a 5" × 31" rectangle on paper. To make the Tail Tuft pattern, draw a 5" × 10" rectangle on paper. Using the Cat Ear and Lion Collar patterns on pages 85 and 88, transfer the patterns onto paper (see General Instructions).

**3.** Using the paper patterns, cut 1 tail piece and 4 ear pieces from beige felt. Cut 1 collar piece and 1 tail tuft piece from rust fur.

**4.** For each ear, stitch or glue 2 felt ear pieces together for added weight and body. Weigh down the ears with some heavy books until they are dry.

**5.** To apply the ears to the hood, pin them at an equal distance from the center of the hood, then glue or stitch them on, leaving 1 to 2 inches of space between the ears.

**6.** For the head opening, cut a circle measuring 7" in diameter from the center of the collar. Slip the collar over the child's head. To adjust overall collar size, trim along the outside edges until the collar is even with the edge of the child's shoulders. When putting on the costume, slip on the collar after the costume but before the hood.

**7.** To make the tail and attach the claws, see steps 7 through 10 of the Curious Cat on pages 3–4. Finally, wrap the tail tuft around the end of the tail and stitch or glue it in place.

### HOW TO ACT LIKE A FEROCIOUS LION

* To let other animals know how proud you are to be a lion, practice a loud roar while shaking your mane.
* To stalk prey, walk quietly and hide in tall grass and bushes. Bend your knees and squat a little while moving 1 paw in front of the other (hand then foot). Put your head forward and always keep a lookout for the enemy, possibly a leopard.
* Take plenty of naps and yawn a lot. Lions sleep almost the whole day—as much as 21 hours! Some sleep in grassy fields and others sleep in caves.
* Lions like to travel in prides (large groups), so be sure to spend plenty of time with your family and friends.

# ELEGANT ELEPHANT

## How to Paint the Face

**1.** Using a damp sponge and Dark Gray #133, cover the entire face.

**2.** Using a medium flat brush and White #000, create "wrinkles" by painting wavy lines across the forehead (down onto the bridge of the nose), eyelids, temples, cheeks, and jawbone.

**3.** Using a medium flat brush and Black #111, trace along 1 side of each "wrinkle," creating a shadowing effect. Then, outline each eye, following closely around the eyelashes.

**4.** Using a medium flat brush and Sparkle Red #55, cover the inner part of the bottom lip.

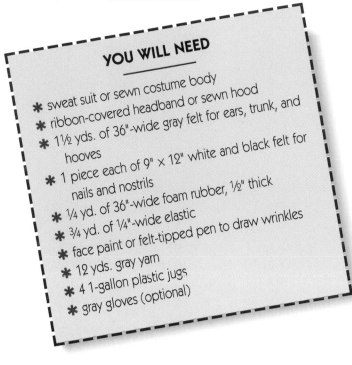

## YOU WILL NEED

* sweat suit or sewn costume body
* ribbon-covered headband or sewn hood
* 1½ yds. of 36"-wide gray felt for ears, trunk, and hooves
* 1 piece each of 9" × 12" white and black felt for nails and nostrils
* ¼ yd. of 36"-wide foam rubber, ½" thick
* ¾ yd. of ¼"-wide elastic
* face paint or felt-tipped pen to draw wrinkles
* 12 yds. gray yarn
* 4 1-gallon plastic jugs
* gray gloves (optional)

## How to Make the Costume

The fastest way to make this costume is by using a hooded sweat suit. To return the suit to normal wear, carefully unstitch the ears and tail.

**1.** Purchase a sweat suit or sew a costume body. Also make a ribbon-covered headband or sew a hood. (See General Instructions.)

**2.** To make the Trunk pattern, draw a 9" × 27" rectangle on paper. To make the Hoof pattern, draw a 13" × 21" rectangle on paper.

**3.** To make the Nostril pattern, draw a circle on paper measuring 3" in diameter. Mark a dot 1" from the circle edge. Draw 2 straight lines from the dot to the outer edges of the circle, creating a teardrop shape. Cut out the pattern following all outside lines.

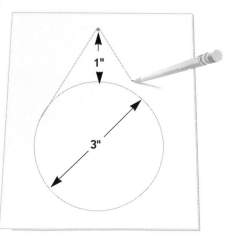

**4.** To make the Nail pattern, draw a 2" × 2" square on paper. Along 1 edge, round off the 2 square corners. Cut out the pattern following all inside lines.

**5.** Using the Elephant Ear pattern on page 86, transfer the pattern onto paper (see General Instructions).

**6.** Using the paper patterns, cut 1 trunk piece, 4 ear pieces, and 4 hoof pieces from gray felt. Cut 2 nostril pieces, one from gray felt and one from black. Cut 16 nail pieces from white felt. Cut 1 trunk piece from the foam rubber.

**7.** With all edges even, glue the felt trunk to the foam trunk. Roll the trunk lengthwise, butting the long foam edges together. Glue the long edges together and then stitch them in place, using long hand stitches.

**8.** With the seam at center, squeeze the trunk at one end to flatten it. Pin each elastic end to the trunk at the folds. Before stitching, try the trunk on the child. It should fit snugly around the back of the head. Alter the length of the elastic as necessary.

**9.** With the seam at the bottom, try the trunk on the child again. Trim the foam area below the elastic strap for comfort if necessary. This area will rest on the upper lip.

**10.** Trim ¾" from all edges of the black felt nostril. Cut the nostril in half lengthwise and glue the halves to the gray nostril, leaving space at the center. Glue the nostril piece to the trunk with the pointed end facing top (opposite the side of the trunk seam). Using face paint or a felt-tipped pen, draw slightly curved lines down the top of the trunk to represent wrinkles.

**11.** To make each ear, glue or stitch 2 felt ear pieces together for added weight and body. With the short straight edge near the top and the long straight edge positioned vertically, hold 1 ear up to the side of the child's head. If necessary, trim along the curved edges to alter the size. Turn under the short straight edge at the top. Pin that edge to the hood and stitch it in place.

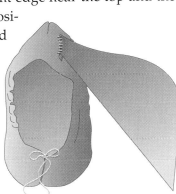

**12.** Wrap the gray yarn around a 10" book or piece of cardboard 40 times. Cut 2 ties, each 8", from the remaining yarn. Thread 1 tie through the top of the wound yarn and tie it. Cut the other end of the wound yarn.

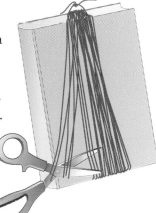

Uncut ends

**13.** Beginning approximately 2" from the tied end, braid the yarn. Secure the braid at the end with the remaining tie. Remove the first tie, spread the uncut ends, and stitch those ends to the seat of the costume.

**14.** To make each hoof, use a craft knife or wire cutter to cut off the top of a plastic jug at the neck. The opening circumference should be a little wider than the child's ankle (approximately 8"). Cut off the handle at the lower edge. Cut a 3" vertical slit from the neck opening to the hole where the handle used to be. Mark a horizontal line halfway up the sides of the jug and cut it in half.

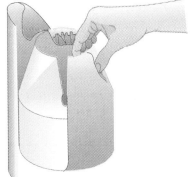

Halfway point

Removed handle

**15.** With several inches of felt extending past the upper and lower edges of the jug, wrap the felt hoof around the jug. Align the short edges of the felt at the jug's vertical slit, trimming the felt if necessary. Glue the felt to the outside of the jug. Tuck any excess felt inside at the upper and lower edges and secure it with glue. Glue 4 nails to the lower front edge (opposite the slit) of each hoof. When putting the costume on, separate the jug at the vertical slit so the child can insert his foot. (Shoes can be put on after the hooves are in place.)

# HOW TO ACT LIKE AN ELEGANT ELEPHANT

✱ An elephant uses its versatile long trunk to sniff for approaching danger, hug another elephant, make trumpet noises, and even take a shower. Swing your trunk back and forth and imagine that you are using your trunk to do these things too.

✱ Have you ever had a baby-sitter? Baby elephants have. A mother elephant will look for a teenage female to baby-sit if she needs to leave for awhile. Help parents you know by offering to baby-sit for them.

✱ Elephants never forget because they love to learn. Like humans, elephants are born with underdeveloped brains. This enables them to learn a lot by watching their parents and relatives. Learn as much as you can from those closest to you. Carefully watch what they do and ask plenty of questions.

✱ Elephant tusks are made from a material similar to that of your teeth. They are usually used for digging, but elephants sometimes use them when charging a predator. When charging, they make a loud and threatening roaring sound to frighten the intruder. Practice your own roaring sounds and see how frightening you can be.

# TERRIFIC TIGER

## How to Paint the Face

**1.** Using a damp sponge and White #000, create circle and color in each eye, covering the eyebrows, the eyelids, and the under-eye area. Next, cover the mouth area, starting at the nostrils, going around the lips, and covering the chin.

**2.** Using a damp sponge and Ochre Yellow #244, cover the center of the forehead, the nose, the under-eye area, and the apples of the cheeks.

**3.** Using a damp sponge and Metallic Copper #755, cover the outer area of the face, starting at the temples, continuing down the outer cheeks and around the jawbone, and finishing under the chin. Blend the metallic copper into the areas with Ochre Yellow #244 using a clean sponge.

**4.** Using a medium flat brush and Black #111, create a "furry snout" by drawing zigzag lines from the outer nostrils to the corners of the mouth. Also, outline the White #000 around the eye area and chin with zigzag lines. Paint the tip of the nose, nostrils, and lips black. Then, paint a line from the tip of the nose to the center of the upper lip. Create "tiger stripes" on the forehead, temples, cheekbones, and chin. Finally, add "whiskers" on the cheeks, "whisker dots" on the upper lip, and short horizontal lines on the bridge of the nose.

## YOU WILL NEED

✻ sweat suit or sewn costume body
✻ ribbon-covered headband or sewn hood
✻ ⅜ yd. of 36"-wide tiger fur for ears and tail
✻ ⅜ yd. of 36"-wide black felt for ears and chest
✻ polyester stuffing
✻ black gloves
✻ black bumpy chenille stems

## How to Make the Costume

If you sew the costume, look for tiger fur or printed tiger felt. If you use a sweat suit, choose a gold color and paint it with narrow black stripes.

**1.** Purchase a sweat suit or sew a costume body. Also make a ribbon-covered headband or sew a felt hood. (See General Instructions.)

**2.** To make the Long Tail pattern, draw a 5" × 31" rectangle on paper. Using the Cat Ear and Cat Chest patterns on page 85, transfer the patterns onto paper (see General Instructions).

**3.** Using the paper patterns, cut 1 tail piece and 4 ear pieces from fur. Cut 2 ear pieces and 1 chest piece from black felt. Trim 1" from the 2 outer curves of the black felt ear pieces to create ear insets.

**4.** Have the child try on the sweatshirt or costume. Carefully pin the chest piece to the front with the wider part at the bottom. Stitch or glue the chest piece in place once the child takes the sweatshirt or costume off.

**5.** For each ear, pin and stitch together 2 fur ear pieces along the curved edges. Turn them right side out and stuff them lightly with polyester stuffing. With bottom edges even, glue the ear inset to the ear front.

**6.** To apply the ears to a hood or head-band, pin them at an equal distance from the center of the hood or band, then glue or stitch them on, leaving 1 to 2 inches of space between the ears.

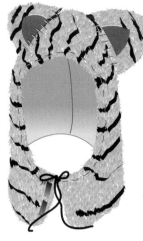

**7.** To make the tail and claws, see steps 7 through 10 of the Curious Cat on pages 3–4.

## HOW TO ACT LIKE A TERRIFIC TIGER

✻ To act like a tiger, look both ways and listen very carefully with your ears standing straight up. Practice this when crossing the street.
✻ If another tiger picks a fight, hiss and expose your fangs and claws. Tigers intimidate before they actually fight.
✻ When you see tigers of the opposite gender, swish your tail slowly to let them know that you like them.
✻ Let other tigers know that your front and back yards belong to you by rubbing against the trees and scratching the bark.

BEES

&

BUGS

# LOVELY LADYBUG

## How to Paint the Face

**1.** Using a damp sponge and Bright Red #0055, cover the face, except the eyelids and under-eye area.

**2.** Using a thin-tip brush and Black #111, cover both eyes, extending the paint onto the eyelids and up near the eyebrows. Paint "ladybug dots" on the cheeks.

**3.** Using a thin-tip brush and Black #111, draw the base of the ladybug antennae, beginning between the eyebrows at the top of the nose and continuing upward and outward to the hairline. Finally, paint the lips.

## YOU WILL NEED

* sweat suit
* antennae headband
* 2 yds. of 36"-wide black felt for sandwich board and legs
* 1¾ yds. of 36"-wide red felt for sandwich board
* 2 pieces of 22" × 28" poster board
* 3¾ yds. of 18"-wide fusible web or fabric glue
* transparent thread
* newspaper to stuff legs
* 2 pairs of gloves

## How to Make the Costume

The sandwich board, made from felt-covered poster board, is worn over the multilegged sweat suit. Black-spotted wings on the back of this costume make it as much fun going as it is coming.

**1.** Purchase a sweat suit and make an antenna headband. (See General Instructions.)

**2.** To determine the length of the felt legs, measure the length of the sweatshirt sleeve. Then, make a paper pattern for them by drawing a rectangle on paper measuring 10" by the sleeve length. Using the paper pattern, cut 2 leg pieces from black felt.

**3.** For each leg, fold the felt piece in half lengthwise and stitch it together along the long edge. Turn the leg inside out so that the right side is on the outside. Cut a sheet of newspaper equal to the leg length. Roll and insert the newspaper into the leg. Crumple additional pieces of newspaper and insert them into the leg to hold its shape.

**4.** Stuff 1 pair of gloves with small, ripped pieces of newspaper. Slip the open end of each glove into a felt leg. With the leg seam facing down and the glove thumb pointing up, stitch the glove to the leg around all edges. Stitch the open end of the leg to the sweatshirt a few inches below the underarm area. Tie a piece of transparent thread snugly around the middle of the felt leg to suggest an elbow. Repeat for the other glove and leg.

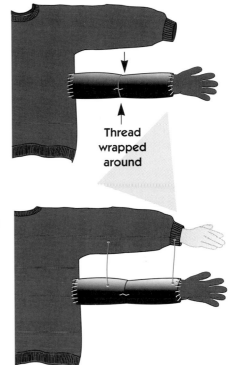

Thread wrapped around

**5.** Using the transparent thread and a large-eyed needle, attach the felt legs to the sweatshirt sleeves at points near the wrists and above the elbows, as shown. Be sure to leave the thread long enough so that the sweatshirt arm and felt leg are parallel. This allows the legs to move with the arms like puppets.

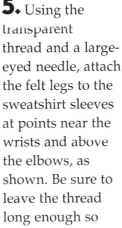

**6.** To determine the sandwich board dimensions, take 2 measurements: For the board length, measure the child from the shoulder at the base of the neck to the knee. For the board width, measure the child from shoulder to shoulder at the widest point. Using these dimensions, cut 2 sandwich boards from poster board.

**7.** With the short edges touching, tape the 2 poster boards together on both sides with masking tape. For the neck opening, cut a hole 7" in diameter, centered on the join. Have the child try on the sandwich board with the join resting on his or her shoulders. Cut the neck opening larger if needed. Measure and mark 2" from 1 outside edge along the join line. Measure and mark 5" on either side of the join line, along the same outside edge. Draw a triangle connecting the marked points, and cut away the piece for a shoulder slope. Use the trimmed triangle as a pattern to trace the slope on the other shoulder.

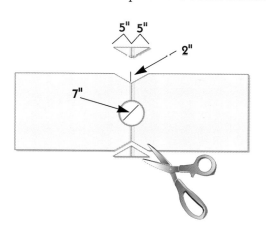

**8.** Measure and mark the center point along 1 of the short uncut ends. Now mark 2 points along the long sides, about 8" from the short end. Draw a curved line connecting 1 side point to the center point. Trim off this corner and use it as a pattern to trim the other corner. Use the 2 trimmed corners as patterns to trace and taper the other end, but position the patterns a few inches in from this short end to make the final lengths of the 2 boards uneven. The shorter length will be the costume front.

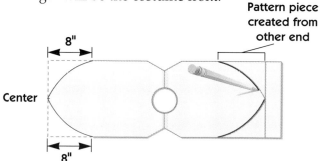

**9.** The felt is attached to the poster board with fusible web or fabric glue. If you're using fusible web, cut 2 pieces, each equal to the full length of the sandwich board. Apply the web to 1 side of

the board near the center, allowing the straight edges of the web to meet near the center but keeping them away from the neck opening. Following the web manufacturer's recommendations for temperature and moisture, fuse the center area of the board first. Trim the outer edges of the web even with the sandwich board edges, and then fuse the rest of the board. Allow the web to cool, then remove the paper backing.

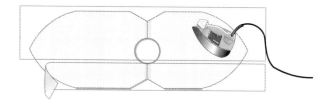

**10.** Cut 1 piece of red felt a few inches wider and longer than the sandwich board. Fuse or glue the felt to the web side of the board. Trim the felt along all edges.

**11.** Turn the board over with the felt side down and apply glue or fusible web (to apply web, see step 9). Cut 1 piece of black felt a few inches wider and longer than the sandwich board. Glue or fuse the felt to this side of the board. Trim the felt along all edges of the board, allowing 1" of felt to extend past the board edges.

**12.** To complete the back wings, make a wing divider pattern by drawing a 6" × 24" rectangle on paper. Mark the center of the rectangle at 1 short end and draw 2 straight lines from the mark to the opposite corners. The center triangle is your pattern. For dots, cut a circle pattern measuring 4" in diameter. Cut out the dot and wing divider patterns following all inside lines. Using the patterns, cut 1 wing divider and 7 dots from black felt and, if fusing, fusible web. If fusing, fuse web to 1 side of the triangle and to 1 side of each of the dots.

**13.** Position the triangle on the center back of the sandwich board with the short straight end extending a few inches below the tapered edge of the red wings.

Trim the triangle even with the tapered edge and fuse or glue it in place.

**14.** Beginning with 1 at the tip of the triangle, fuse the dots to the back wings.

**15.** To put the costume on, put on the multi-legged sweat suit and then pull the sandwich board on over the head.

## HOW TO ACT LIKE A LOVELY LADYBUG

✳ Ladybugs help us with our food supply. Inform those around you that while ladybugs are pretty to look at, they also eat aphids, insects, and plant lice—all creatures that can ruin farmers crops if they are left to roam around.

✳ Ladybugs are also called lady beetles, ladybirds, and ladybird beetles. Select which of these names is your favorite, then see if those around you select the same name too.

# BEAUTIFUL BUTTERFLY

## How to Paint the Face

**1.** Using a large flat brush and Black #111, draw an oval outline around each eye. Draw slightly larger ovals around the first 2 ovals, making sure the larger ovals meet at the bridge of the nose. Outline 2 teardrops at the center of the forehead and 4 teardrops on the lower jawbone. Fill in the inner oval around each eye. Then, cover the rest of the face, starting at the 2 larger ovals and staying outside of the teardrop outlines.

**2.** Using a medium flat brush and Bright Pink #0058, color in the oval outlines around the eyes.

**3.** First, using a medium flat brush and Sparkle Turquoise #48, color in 1 teardrop on the forehead and 2 teardrops on the jaw, leaving an unpainted teardrop next to each one you paint. Now, using a medium flat brush and Sparkle Lilac #87, fill in the remaining 3 teardrops.

**4.** Using a medium flat brush and White #000, draw "honeycombs" in the ovals around the eyes to create butterfly eyes.

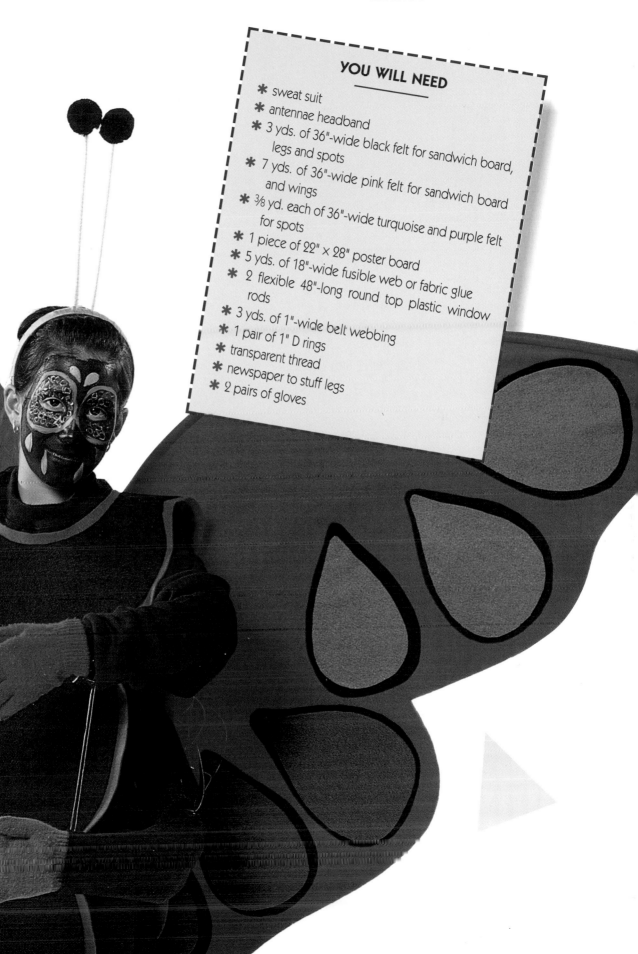

## YOU WILL NEED

* sweat suit
* antennae headband
* 3 yds. of 36"-wide black felt for sandwich board, legs and spots
* 7 yds. of 36"-wide pink felt for sandwich board and wings
* ⅜ yd. each of 36"-wide turquoise and purple felt for spots
* 1 piece of 22" x 28" poster board
* 5 yds. of 18"-wide fusible web or fabric glue
* 2 flexible 48"-long round top plastic window rods
* 3 yds. of 1"-wide belt webbing
* 1 pair of 1" D rings
* transparent thread
* newspaper to stuff legs
* 2 pairs of gloves

## How to Make the Costume

Butterflies come in many colors, so mix and match the felt wings and sweat suit colors however you wish. An additional pair of legs is made from felt and stitched to the sweatshirt sides. Butterfly wings keep their shape with flexible curtain rods and are then belted around the sweatshirt, under a felt-covered poster board.

**1.** Purchase a sweat suit and make an antenna headband. (See General Instructions.)

**2.** To assemble the legs, see steps 2 through 5 of the Lovely Ladybug on page 29.

**3.** To determine the dimensions of the sandwich board, take 2 measurements: For the board length, measure the child from the shoulder at the base of the neck to the knee. For the board width, measure the child from shoulder to shoulder at the widest point. Using these dimensions, cut a sandwich board pattern from paper.

**4.** To create the scalloped butterfly shape, divide 1 long edge into 3 equal sections, measuring and marking those sections 2" in from the long edge. Draw scallops alternating from the section marks to the side edge of the board. On 1 short edge, mark the center of the paper. Draw a line from the last scallop to the mark. Fold the paper in half lengthwise and trace the scallops on the opposite side. Cut along all lines (the last half-scallop on either side will fall away).

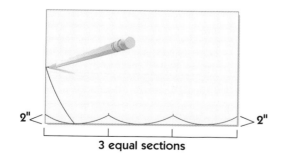

2"          2"

**3 equal sections**

**5.** Using the paper pattern, trace and cut the same shape from poster board. With the short edges touching, tape the paper and poster board together on both sides using masking tape. For the neck opening, cut a hole 7" in diameter, centered on the join. Have the child try on the sandwich board with the join resting on his or her shoulders. Cut the neck opening larger if needed.

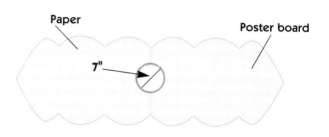

Paper                                    Poster board

7"

**6.** Following steps 9 through 11 of the Lovely Ladybug on page 30, attach the felt to the poster board with fusible web or fabric glue. For the outside of the sandwich board, substitute black for red felt. For the lining (attached to the other side), substitute pink for black felt. Also, remember that the sandwich board for this costume is poster board on the front but paper on the back.

**7.** Transfer the Butterfly Wing and Butterfly Spot patterns on page 86 onto paper (see General Instructions). Also, create a border spot pattern by adding ¾" to all edges of the spot pattern. Using the paper patterns, cut 4 wings from pink felt and 6 spots each from turquoise and purple felt. Cut 12 border spots from black felt. If fusing, cut 12 spots and 12 border spots from fusible web.

**8.** For each wing, pin and stitch together the long curved edges of 2 wing pieces. Trim the seam allowance to ¼" and turn the wing to the right side. Measure and mark a stitching line 1" from seam for the curtain rod

Right side of butterfly wing

1"

casing. Stitch through both layers along the marked line.

**9.** If fusing, fuse web to 1 side of all spots. Fuse the black spots to the wing, then center and fuse a colored spot on each black spot. Give the wings an artistic touch by repositioning the spots, altering the spots' size or edging, or applying more spots to the backs of the wings.

**10.** Slide 1 curtain rod into each casing, trimming the rod if necessary. At each casing end, stitch the felt together with a few strong stitches to prevent the rod from slipping out. Beginning at the lower end of the rods, hand stitch the wings together as far up as possible (approximately 12" to 15"), to the point where they begin to separate.

**11.** Ask someone to hold the wings against the child's back. At the center-stitched area, mark the wings at the child's waistline and at the shoulder blades, no higher than the underarm areas. Cut the belting in half, slip 1 end of each belt through a pair of D rings, and stitch securely. Pin and stitch each belt to the wings, where marked.

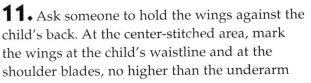
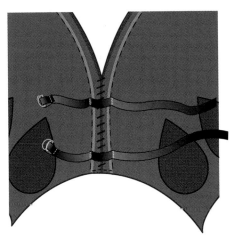

**12.** When dressing, have the child put on the multilegged sweat suit first, followed by the sandwich board, with the softer side in back and the stiffer side in front. Have someone hold up the front of the board, while you strap the wings over the board in the back and under the board in the front.

## HOW TO ACT LIKE A BEAUTIFUL BUTTERFLY

* Butterflies come in many colors, so be creative when making your costume: Choose orange and black to look like a monarch butterfly, blue and gold to look like a common blue butterfly, or white to look like a gypsy moth.

* Butterflies have a varied diet. Some eat the juicy center of plant stems, some eat fruit and seeds, and others, like honeybees, eat the sweet nectar of flowers. Eat like a butterfly by including many different foods in your diet.

# TERRIBLE TARANTULA

## How to Paint the Face

**1.** Using a damp sponge and Metallic Copper #755, paint a circle in each mouth corner. Then, beginning from these corners, extend the color down each side of the chin to form curved "fangs." Cover the forehead, down the center of the nose to the tip, across the middles of the cheeks, up through the temples to the forehead, and down across the apples of the cheeks to the corners of the mouth.

**2.** Using a damp sponge and Black #111, cover the unpainted areas of the face. Using a clean sponge with no paint, blend or "feather" the black into the copper areas.

**3.** Using a medium round brush and Black #111, define the copper "fangs" at the corners of the mouth and bring them to a point. Paint tiny dots on the apples of the cheeks. Paint lines along the eyelashes. Create "spider fur" by making tiny slashes across the forehead and cheeks, on the chin, and around the mouth.

**4.** Using a medium round brush and Metallic Copper #755, create "spider fur" on the cheeks and chin with small dashed lines. Finally, using a medium round brush and White #000, add small dots to the black areas under the eyes and the black circles across the cheeks.

## How to Make the Costume

A felt sandwich board rests on the shoulders over the 8 spider legs. The first pair of legs are a felt extension of the sweatshirt sleeves. The second and third pairs are made from felt and attached to the sides of the sweatshirt and pants. Legs are then strung together with transparent thread so they can move with the arms like puppets.

**1.** Purchase a sweat suit. Also, purchase a knit hat or sew a hood. (See General Instructions.)

**2.** To determine the length of the felt legs, measure the length of the sweatshirt sleeve. To make a paper pattern for them, draw a rectangle on paper measuring 10" by 1½ times the measured sleeve length. Using the paper pattern, cut 6 leg pieces from black felt. Trim 2 of the felt pieces to ⅓ of their original length. These 2 short pieces will be the top pair of legs, which are just extensions of the sweatshirt sleeves.

**3.** To make the leg joint pattern, draw a 2" × 18" rectangle on paper. Using the paper pattern, cut 8 pieces from rust felt. Transfer the Tarantula Foot pattern on page 84 onto paper (see General Instructions). Using the paper pattern, cut 12 foot pieces from rust felt.

**4.** For each leg, fold the felt piece in half lengthwise and stitch together along the long edge. Turn the leg inside out so that the right side is on the outside. Cut a sheet of newspaper equal to the leg length. Roll and insert the newspaper into the leg. Crumple additional pieces of newspaper and insert them into the leg to help hold its shape.

**5.** For each leg, stitch together the curved edges of 2 spider foot pieces, pivoting at the point. Turn the foot inside out so that the right side is on the outside. Stuff lightly with newspaper.

**6.** Slip 1 end of each leg into the open end of a spider foot. Stitch or glue the leg to the foot along all edges. For the longer, lower legs, stitch the open end of 1 leg pair to the sweatshirt below the arms and 1 pair to the sweatpants at the sides, approximately 6" below the waistband. For accurate and even leg spacing, have the child try on the sweat suit or costume body.

**7.** For each top leg, slip the open end of the short leg over the end of the sweatshirt cuff. Stitch the leg to the sleeve, leaving the back open. This opening will allow the child to slip his or her hand in

and out of the leg easily for safety and comfort.

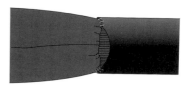

**8.** Wrap a leg joint strip around the sweatshirt cuff area. Stitch the short edges of the strip together, trimming the strip to fit if necessary. Stitch 1 long edge of the joint to the sweatshirt sleeve all the way around. Stitch the other long edge of the joint to the felt leg in the front only, leaving the back open so the child's hand can still be inserted through the opening.

**9.** With the child wearing the sweatshirt, position another joint on each sweatshirt sleeve, pulling the joint taut to create a slight indent. Stitch or glue these joints to the sleeve. Stitch or glue 2 leg joints to the rest of the legs (even the legs on the sweatpants!) spacing them to match the joints on the arms.

**10.** Using the transparent thread and a large-eyed needle, string the arms and attached legs together at the joints and feet. Leave the thread long enough to keep the legs parallel, so they will move with the arms like puppets. To simplify dressing, string the thread for the third pair of legs through a safety pin and pin, rather than stitch, the thread to the above leg. This will allow the sweatshirt and sweatpants to remain separate.

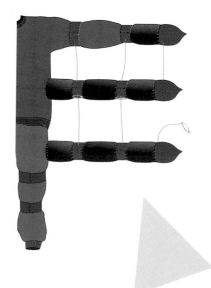

**11.** To determine the dimensions of the sandwich board, take 2 measurements: For the board length, measure the child from the shoulder at the base of the neck to the knee. For the board width, measure the child from shoulder to shoulder at the widest point. Using these dimensions, cut 2 sandwich boards from poster board.

**12.** With the short edges touching, tape the 2 poster boards together on both sides using masking tape. For the neck opening, cut a hole 7" in diameter, centered on the join of the boards. To double-check the size of the neck opening, have the child try on the sandwich board with the join resting on his or her shoulders. Cut the opening larger if needed. Measure and mark 2" from 1 outside edge of the board along the join line then and 5" on either side of the join line along the same outside edge. Draw a triangle connecting the marked points and cut away the piece for a shoulder slope. Use the trimmed triangle as a pattern to trace the slope on the other shoulder.

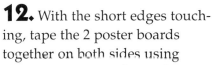

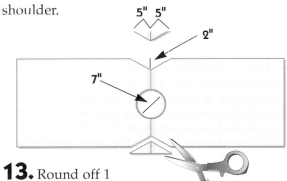

**13.** Round off 1 lower corner of the board and cut along the line. Use the trimmed corner as a pattern to trace and round off the other corners.

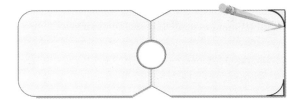

**14.** Following steps 9 through 11 of the Lovely Ladybug on page 30, attach the felt to the poster board with fusible web or fabric glue. For the outside of the sandwich board, use rust felt instead of red. Use black felt for the lining, which is attached to the other side of the board.

## HOW TO ACT LIKE A TERRIBLE TARANTULA

* The many varieties of spiders live anywhere from the seaside to the mountains, yet they all weave webs to catch their prey. Once a spider catches something in its web, the spider either crushes it with its powerful leg muscles or stings it with its poisonous venom. Pretend you are crushing prey by giving someone a gentle hug with the six attached legs of your costume.

* All spiders have 8 legs, 2 main body portions, no antennae, and no teeth. Therefore, what we call a spider bite is either a sting or pinch from their sharp claws. Give make-believe spider "pinches" by brushing someone softly with the felt claws of your costume.

# BUSY BUMBLEBEE

## How to Paint the Face

**1.** Using a damp sponge and Bright Yellow #222, cover the face, including the tip of the nose and nostrils but excluding the nose, eyebrows, eyelids, and under-eye area.

**2.** Using a large flat brush and Black #111, cover the areas left unpainted in step 1. Paint tiny slash marks around the outline of the "mask" and then over the areas covered with Bright Yellow #222. Paint the lips. Create "jaw antennae," extending from the outer nostrils through the corners of the mouth down to the jawbone.

**3.** Using a medium flat brush and White #000, draw a large circle around each eye, inside the mask area. Then, paint other tiny circles within these circles to create bumblebee eyes. Lightly paint the inside of the "jaw antennae." Finally, make tiny slash marks around the outside of the larger white circles.

## YOU WILL NEED

* sweat suit
* antennae headband
* 2 yds. of 36"-wide black felt for sandwich board and legs
* ¾ yd. of 36"-wide yellow felt for sandwich board
* ¼ yd. of 36"-wide white felt for tail
* ⅝ yd. of 45"-wide lightweight black fabric for wings
* 4 yds. of 24-gauge wire
* 2 pieces of 22" x 28" poster board
* 4 yds. of 18"-wide fusible web or fabric glue
* transparent thread
* newspaper to stuff legs
* 2 pairs of gloves

## How to Make the Costume

The sandwich board, which is made from poster board, is covered with black and yellow felt and is worn over a multilegged sweat suit.

**1.** Purchase a sweat suit and make an antennae headband. (See General Instructions.)

**2.** To assemble the legs, see steps 2 through 5 of the Lovely Ladybug on page 29.

**3.** To determine the dimensions of the sandwich board, take 2 measurements: For the board length, measure the child from the shoulder at the base of the neck to the knee. For the board width, measure the child from shoulder to shoulder at the widest point. Using these dimensions, cut 2 sandwich boards from poster board.

**4.** With the short edges touching, tape the 2 poster boards together on both sides using masking tape. For the neck opening, cut a hole 7" in diameter, centered on the join. Have the child try on the sandwich board with the join resting on his or her shoulders. Cut the neck opening larger if needed. Measure and mark 2" from 1 outside edge of the sandwich board along the join line and 5" on either side of the join line along the same outside edge. Draw a triangle connecting the marked points and cut away the piece for a shoulder slope. Use the trimmed triangle as a pattern to trace the slope on the other shoulder.

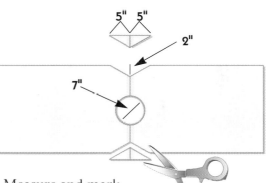

**5.** Measure and mark the center point along 1 of the short uncut ends. Now mark 2 points along the long sides, about 8" from the short end. Draw a curved line connecting 1 side point to the center point. Trim off this corner and use it as a pattern to trim the other corner. Use the 2 trimmed corners as patterns to trace and taper the other end, but position the patterns a few inches in from this short end to make the final lengths of the 2 boards uneven. The shorter length will be the costume front.

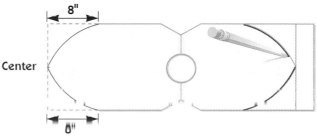

**6.** Following steps 9 through 11 of the Lovely Ladybug on page 30, attach the felt to the poster board with fusible web or fabric glue, using black felt to cover both the outside and the lining of the poster board. Trim the edges of both felt covers even with the edges of the poster board leaving no 1" extension.

**7.** For stripes and the tail, make a pattern by drawing a 5" × 24" rectangle on paper. Using the paper pattern, cut 4 stripes from yellow felt, 1 tail from white felt, and, if fusing, 5 pieces from fusible web. If fusing, fuse the web to 1 side of all felt rectangles.

**8.** With the short edges parallel to sides of the board, position the tail on the center back (remember, the back is the longer side) of the sandwich board with 1 long edge of the tail even with the tapered point of the board. Following the tapered point, trace and trim the tail even with the lower edge of the board. Fuse or glue the tail to the back over the black felt.

**9.** Place 2 yellow stripes into position on the back of the board parallel to and above the tail and spaced evenly. If necessary, trim the short side edges even with the board edges. Fuse the stripes to the back. Then, position, trim, and fuse 2 stripes to the front board.

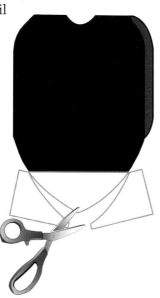

**10.** Transfer the Bee Wing pattern on page 87 onto paper (see General Instructions). Using the paper pattern, cut 4 wing pieces from black fabric. Cut the wire into 4 pieces. To make 1 wing, pin and stitch together 2 wing pieces along the shaped edge, keeping all edges even. Begin and end stitching ½" from the straight edge of the fabric. Turn the wing inside out so that the right side is on the outside; press flat. Repeat for the other wing.

**11.** For each wing, place 2 lengths of wire between the layers of fabric up against the stitched seam. Stitch the wires in place against the seam, by hand or with a sewing machine. Trim the ends even with the fabric edge. Then, stitch the wing together ½" from the straight edge.

**12.** Open the seam allowances along the straight edge and bend the wires at each corner so that they are open too. Press the seam allowance open. On either side of the center of the back of the sandwich board, draw 2 parallel vertical lines, approximately 12" long and 5" apart. Apply glue to the pressed seam allowances and attach the wings to the board along the marked lines. Allow the wings to dry.

**13.** When dressing, have the child put on the multilegged sweat suit first and then pull the sandwich board on over his or her head.

## HOW TO ACT LIKE A BUSY BUMBLEBEE

* Bumblebees are the biggest and usually the noisiest of all bees. The buzzing noise comes from their flapping wings, but you can imitate it another way. Practice making bee sounds with your mouth and see how noisy you can be.
* Bumblebees nest in the ground and honey bees nest in the trees. Both make honey but the sweeter and tastier type that we eat is made by honey bees. Have you ever had honey? Taste some!
* Bees are a friend to all flowers, and gardeners love them. They carry pollen made by the male flowers to the female flowers, which allows more flowers to be made. This is called pollination. For added effect, carry flowers as part of your costume.

EXOTIC FAVORITES

# PLAYFUL PANDA

## How to Paint the Face

**1.** First, using a damp sponge and White #000, cover the face, excluding the eyelids, eyebrows, and under-eye area. Then, using a new, damp sponge and Light Gray #122, apply a shade of gray over the white. Concentrate the light gray on the upper forehead, upper lip, chin, and jawbone around the ear. Lightly blend the white and light gray paints.

**2.** Using a medium flat brush and Black #111, cover the eyelids, eyebrows, and under eye area, creating asymmetrical triangles around the eyes. Paint the tip of the nose, the nostrils, and the area just below the nose in the shape of an upside-down triangle. Paint the bottom lip and have the child rub his or her lips together.

**3.** Using a medium flat brush and Black #111, paint a tiny triangle just below the point of the upside-down triangle. Create a "snout" with lines that curve from the outer nostrils around to the corners of the mouth. Then, draw 2 curved lines evenly spaced on either side of the lower lip and extending down to the lower edge of the chin. Finally, add "whisker dots" to the snout.

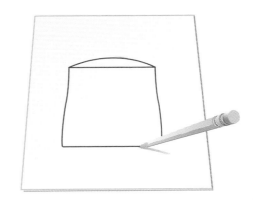

## How to Make the Costume

Choose fuzzy plush felt for the white midriff and hood and black plush felt for the ears. Sew the midriff to a black felt costume body or a black sweatshirt. For the most authentic-looking costume, attach the ears to a sewn hood rather than a headband.

**1.** Purchase a sweat suit or sew a costume body. Also sew a hood. (See General Instructions.)

**2.** Transfer the Panda Ear pattern on page 85 onto paper (see General Instructions).

**3.** To make the midriff pattern, place the felt costume or sweatshirt flat on a table. Trace the side edges from the underarms to the height of the crotch or to the lower edge of the sweatshirt.

**4.** Remove the costume and complete the pattern by drawing 2 horizontal lines to connect the upper and lower ends, respectively. Reshape the upper edge to show a slight rise in the center. Cut out the pattern along the outside lines.

**5.** Using the paper patterns, cut 4 ear pieces from black felt and 2 midriff pieces from white felt.

**6.** With the right sides facing, pin and stitch together both side edges of the midriff pieces. Turn the sewn midriff piece inside out so that the right side is on the outside.

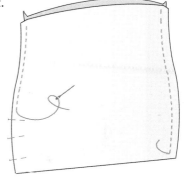

**7.** If you're using a sweatshirt, slip the midriff piece over the bottom end, up to the underarms. Then, pin and stitch it to the sweatshirt along the top and bottom edges.

**8.** If you're using a felt costume, slip the midriff piece over the bottom end, up to the underarms. Then, pin and stitch the top and bottom edges to the costume in the front only. Turn the costume over to show the back. Cut a vertical rectangle in the midriff back to expose the costume's zipper. Pin and stitch

Back of the costume

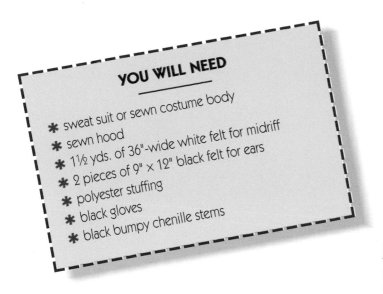

the upper and lower edges of the midriff to the costume back. Also, pin and stitch the edges of the rectangular opening to the costume back to make the zipper accessible.

**9.** For each ear, pin and stitch together 2 felt ear pieces along the long curved edges. Turn the ear inside out so that the right side is on the outside. Stuff slightly with polyester filling. To apply the ears to the hood, pin them at an equal distance from the center of the hood, then glue or stitch them on, leaving 2" to 3" of space between the ears.

**10.** To make the claws, see step 10 of the Curious Cat on page 4.

## HOW TO ACT LIKE A PLAYFUL PANDA

* Practice your somersaults, especially in slow motion, because panda cubs are expert tumblers.
* Pandas can eat as much as 40 pounds of bamboo leaves in a day. To imitate a panda, eat plenty of green leafy vegetables, but no bamboo leaves, please.
* Pandas are generally quiet animals. When they fight, which is not very often, they make low growling sounds. Be very quiet, then surprise those who approach you by letting out a low growl.

# PARENTAL PENGUIN

## How to Paint the Face

**1.** Using a damp sponge and Bright Yellow #222, cover the outer cheeks and jawbone and under the chin.

**2.** First, using a damp sponge and White #000, cover the eyebrows, eyelids, and under-eye areas. Then, using a medium flat brush, draw a thick line on each side of the nose and down the center of the nose. Next, draw a curved line below the nose, from outer nostril to outer nostril, and fill in the area. Draw a thick line from the left lower cheek, below the bottom lip, and out to the right lower cheek. Fill in the area between the line and the bottom lip, covering the lip.

**3.** Using a large flat brush and Black #111, color in all unpainted areas of the face, but be careful not to blend the colors.

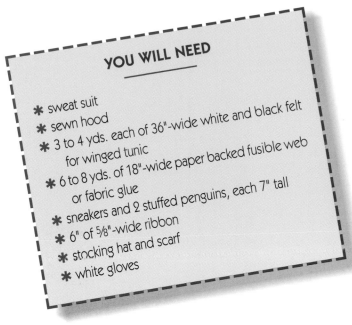

## How to Make the Costume

While the best choice for this costume is a white sweat suit and a winged tunic, you can also use a sewn costume body underneath the winged tunic. Carrying baby penguins and wearing a hat and scarf are optional, but they're probably too much fun to eliminate.

**1.** Purchase a sweat suit or sew a costume body. Also sew a hood. (See General Instructions.)

**2.** To make the winged tunic, Bird Tunic and Bird Wing patterns are provided in 3 sizes on pages 87 and 88. To determine the proper size, measure the child's chest and hips, then choose from the chart below. To measure the chest, view the child from the side and measure the fullest part above the waist. To measure the hips, view the child from the side and measure the fullest part below the waist. For both measurements, make sure the tape is parallel with the floor. Transfer the patterns onto paper in the determined size (see General Instructions).

### Bird Tunic and Wing Pattern Size Chart

| Pattern Size | Chest Measurement | Hip Measurement |
|---|---|---|
| Small | 21"–24" | 22"–26" |
| Medium | 24"–27" | 26"–29" |
| Large | 27"–30" | 29"–33" |

**3.** To determine the proper lengths, take 2 measurements: For the tunic length, measure the child at center front from the base of the neck to the middle of the shin. For the wing length, measure the child from the side of the base of the neck to the wrist.

**4.** If necessary, alter the length of the tunic or wing. First, mark the paper pattern with a horizontal line near the center (as shown), and then add or subtract inches at that line. For example, to lengthen the tunic, cut along the line to split the pattern and add a piece of paper the determined number of inches. To shorten the wing, fold the pattern along the line and subtract the determined number of inches. Once altered, even up the cutting lines at the sides of the pattern.

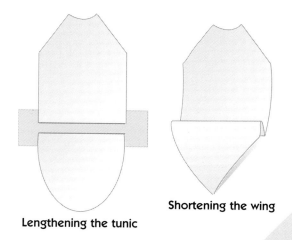

Lengthening the tunic

Shortening the wing

**5.** Using the paper patterns, cut 2 tunic and 2 wing pieces from white felt and 2 of each from black felt. Pair up the 2 white tunic pieces for the front, the 2 black tunic pieces for the back. Then match 1 white wing and 1 black wing piece for each side. Glue the paired pieces together, or attach them using fusible web (see steps 6 through 8).

**6.** To adhere the front tunic pieces together using the fusible web, cut 2 pieces of web, each equal to the tunic length. Allowing the straight edges of the web to meet at the center, apply the web to the wrong side of 1 tunic at the center, following the manufacturer's recommendations for temperature and moisture. Fuse the center area first. Then trim the web even with the felt tunic and continue fusing along the edges. Allow the web to cool and then remove the paper backing.

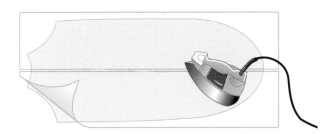

**7.** With the applied web between the felt layers, fuse together the 2 front tunics with wrong sides facing and all edges even.

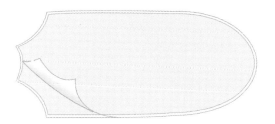

**8.** Repeat the fusing process for the back tunics and wings. To conserve web, cut only 3 lengths equal to the length of the wing. Cut 1 length in half lengthwise and use 1½ lengths for each wing pair, allowing the straight edge of the web to meet off center.

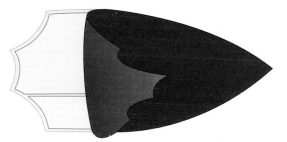

**9.** Using an air soluble marking pen, mark a ½" seam line along the straight edges of the front and back tunics on the right side (color worn outside) of the felt.

**10.** For each wing, make sure that the neck edges are even and the right sides are facing up. Then, pin a wing to the front tunic, keeping the straight edge of the wing aligned with the marked line of the tunic. Apply 2 rows of hand or machine stitches, 1 along the wing edge and 1 along the tunic edge. Turn the assembly over to stitch the second row. Repeat to attach the other wing an then the back tunic piece.

**11.** Have the child try on the tunic. If the neck opening is too small, remove the garment and trim the opening slightly or cut a short slit in the center back.

**12.** To attach 1 stuffed penguin to a sneaker, first cut 2 pieces of ribbon, each 1½" long. Turn it under ¼" on the cut edges. Pin both ribbons to the bottom of the penguin, 1 near the front and 1 near the back. Stitch the ribbon securely to the penguin along the folds.

**Bottom of stuffed penguin**

**13.** For each stuffed penguin, remove the shoelace from the sneaker and thread it through the front ribbon loop. Lace up the sneaker to the last pair of holes. Then, thread each shoelace tail through the back ribbon loop approaching from opposite ends and then through the last pair of shoelace holes.

## HOW TO ACT LIKE A PARENTAL PENGUIN

* Put the heels of your feet together with your toes pointed outward to practice waddling like a penguin. Both mom and dad penguins carry the babies on their feet to keep them warm and up off the icy floor.
* Penguins are excellent swimmers who like to hunt for fish. Be a healthy penguin at mealtime and put in a special request for fish.

# MIGHTY STEGOSAURUS

## How to Paint the Face

**1.** Using a damp sponge and Grass Green #477, cover the forehead, temples, outer cheeks, upper cheeks, nose, nostrils, area below the nose, and jawbone. Also cover the area under the chin.

**2.** Using a medium round brush and White #000, create teeth within the unpainted "dinosaur mouth" area. The teeth should be staggered on the top and bottom so they fit in between each other. Begin the "dinosaur eyes" near the inner corners of the child's eyes and paint outward. Bring each eye to a point near the temples, leaving a small outline of unpainted skin from above the inner eyebrows to the inner corners of the eyes.

**3.** Using a medium round brush and Bright Red #0055, fill in the unpainted area around each tooth. Also, fill in the unpainted area near the inner corners of the eyes.

**4.** Using a medium round brush and Dark Green #455, outline the "dinosaur mouth." Make a small triangle at the center of the upper lip. Draw a thick line above the white "dinosaur eyes" and extending down next to the red corners of the eyes. Finally, create "wrinkles" by drawing wavy horizontal lines around the outside of the mouth, under the eyes on the cheeks, across the nose, across the forehead, and under the chin.

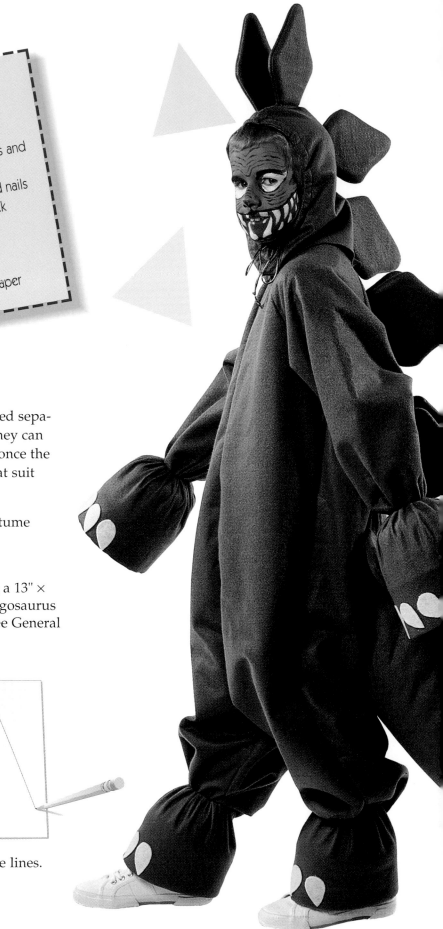

## YOU WILL NEED

* ✱ sweat suit or sewn costume body
* ✱ sewn hood
* ✱ 5 yds. of 36"-wide green felt, for tail, plates and hooves
* ✱ ½ yd. of 36"-wide white felt for spikes and nails
* ✱ 1¼ yds. of 36"-wide foam rubber, ½" thick
* ✱ 1½ yds. of ⅝"-wide grosgrain ribbon
* ✱ polyester stuffing
* ✱ 4 plastic 1-gallon jugs
* ✱ 3 sheets of 20" × 30" wrapping tissue paper

## How to Make the Costume

The tail, hooves, and hood are assembled separately from the costume body so that they can be easily removed from the sweat suit once the party is over. Match the felt to the sweat suit color as closely as possible.

**1.** Purchase a sweat suit or sew a costume body. Also sew a hood. (See General Instructions.)

**2.** Make the hoof pattern by drawing a 13" × 21" rectangle on paper. Transfer the Stegosaurus Plate pattern on page 88 onto paper (see General Instructions).

**3.** To make the tail pattern, draw a 9" × 40" rectangle on paper. To make the spike pattern, draw a 4" × 10" rectangle on paper. For each pattern, mark the center of the rectangle at 1 short end. Draw 2 straight lines from the center mark to the opposite corners. Cut out the patterns following all inside lines. The center triangle is the pattern.

**4.** To make the nail pattern, draw a 1½" × 2" rectangle on paper. At 1 short end, round off the 2 corners of the rectangle. At the opposite short end, mark the center of the rectangle. Draw 2 lines from the center mark to the rounded corners, creating a teardrop shape.

**5.** Using the paper patterns, cut 3 tail pieces, 36 plate pieces, and 4 hoof pieces from green felt. Cut 8 spike pieces and 16 nail pieces from white felt. Cut eighteen 9" squares from foam and eighteen 10" squares from tissue paper.

**6.** With all edges even, pin and stitch together 1 long edge of 2 tail pieces. With short edges and pointed ends even, pin and stitch the open long edges to the remaining tail piece. Turn the tail inside out so that the right side is on the outside.

**7.** With 1 seam at the upper edge and the remaining seams matching, place the tail flat on a table. Measure along the lower folded edge, approximately 6" from the opening and mark. Draw a straight line from the mark to the corner of the upper seam and trim the tail through both layers along the line.

6"

**8.** Stuff the tail halfway with polyester stuffing. Have the child put on the costume or sweatpants. Hold the tail at the corner of the upper seam and hold it up to the child at the seat of the sweatpants or costume body (below the costume zipper). With tail in this position, approximately ⅓ of the tail should drag on the floor. The upper tail seam should match the center back seam of the sweatpants or costume. Trim at the open edge to alter the tail angle and tail length as necessary.

**9.** Have the child take the costume off. Finish stuffing the tail and then pin the tail to the pants or costume, matching the upper tail seam to the pant or costume center back seam. Next, attach the tail using large hand stitches.

**10.** Cut the ribbon in half. Locate the tail placement inside the costume (look for the hand stitches). Inside the costume, stitch 1 end of each ribbon to each side of the tail base (unlike the illustration, your tail does not yet have plates or spikes attached to it). When putting the costume on, the child should slip into the legs first. Then, the ribbon is tied around his or her waist to help support the weight of the tail. Finally, pull up the remainder of the costume, covering the tied ribbon.

**11.** To make each plate, layer 1 square of tissue paper, 1 square of foam, and 2 pieces of felt on the table. Keep all felt edges even and allow the straight edges to extend ½" past the foam edges. Allow the tissue paper to extend past the foam and felt edges. Because the tissue is there to prevent the foam from binding on the metal sewing machine, eliminate it if you are sewing by hand.

Tissue paper

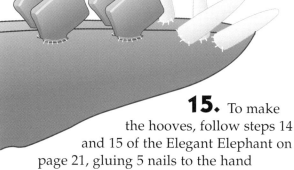
Foam

½"

**12.** Pin through all layers around the curved edges of the plate. Stitch a ¼" seam, beginning and ending at the edge of the foam. Tear away the tissue paper and trim the foam along the curved edges of the felt. Reach between the felt layers and turn the plate to the right side. Repeat for all remaining plates.

**13.** For each spike, stitch together 2 spike pieces along both long edges with a ¼"

seam. Trim the seam close to the point, and turn the spike inside out so that the right side is on the outside. Then, stuff it with polyester stuffing.

**14.** Working in pairs, pin the plates and spikes down the center back of the costume, ½" on either side of the center back seam. Pin 3 pairs of plates to the hood, 2 pairs to the costume body or sweatshirt, and 4 pairs to the tail. Pin 2 pairs of spikes to the end of the tail. Hand stitch or glue the plates and spikes in place. To help plates stand up, open the lower seam allowance and apply glue to the lower edge of the foam as well as to the felt.

**15.** To make the hooves, follow steps 14 and 15 of the Elegant Elephant on page 21, gluing 5 nails to the hand hooves and 3 nails to the feet hooves.

---

## HOW TO ACT LIKE A MIGHTY STEGOSAURUS

* The stegosaurus lived 135 million years ago during the Jurassic period. Although it weighed 2 tons and measured 20 feet long, it ate only plants. To act like a stegosaurus, walk very slowly on all 4 legs and eat plenty of greens.
* The stegosaurus probably used the spikes at the end of its tail as a weapon. Swing your tail gently from side to side to protect yourself from others who try to sneak up behind you.

# EERIE VAMPIRE BAT

## How to Paint the Face

**1.** First, using a damp sponge and Beige Brown #911, cover the eyelids, eyebrows, under-eye areas, nose, nostrils, area under the nose, and inner apples of the cheeks. Next, using a medium flat brush, paint an exaggerated smile across the lips and beyond the outer corners of the mouth.

**2.** Using a medium flat brush and White #000, create triangular fangs on the bottom lip.

**3.** Using a medium flat brush and Black #111, outline the tip of the nose and paint triangles that start at the nostrils. Outline the eyes and nose and around the lips. Cover the forehead, temples, cheeks, jawbone, upper lip, and chin. Outline the fangs. Finally, draw a line across the eyelid and around the eyelashes for emphasis.

**4.** Using a thin-tip brush and White #000, make tiny slashes over the outer areas of the face, including the forehead, chin, and area under the nose. Draw a curved line above and below the outer eyes.

## YOU WILL NEED

* sweat suit or sewn costume body
* ribbon-covered headband or sewn hood
* 1½ yds. of 72"-wide black felt for wings and ears
* ⅜ yd. of 36"-wide beige felt for bones and ear insets
* 40" of 24-gauge wire
* black gloves
* black felt-tip pen

## How to Make the Costume

If you use a sweat suit, stitch the wings on using long stitches, rather than glue, to allow for easy removal afterward.

**1.** Purchase a sweat suit or sew a costume body. Also make a ribbon-covered headband or sew a felt hood. (See General Instructions.)

**2.** To make the bat wing pattern, take 2 measurements: For the wing span, have the child stand with his or her arms held straight out at shoulder height, parallel to the floor. With the tape measure placed horizontally across his or her back, measure from wrist to wrist. For the wing height, position the tape measure vertically and measure from the base of the neck to the top of the shoe.

**3.** Using these 2 measurements, draw a T shape on a large piece of paper. Connect the ends of the T to form a double triangle.

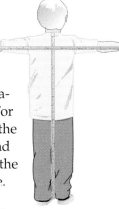

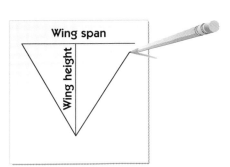

**4.** Beginning at the intersection of the T, draw 2 straight lines dividing each triangle half into thirds, creating 6 triangle wedges.

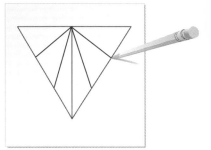

**5.** To complete the wing pattern, draw a curved scallop between each wedged section. Cut out the pattern along the top of the T and the scalloped edges.

**6.** For the skeleton bones, cut 7 strips of paper, each 1½" wide. You should have 1 strip for each of the 5 dividing lines on the wings and 1 strip for each costume sleeve. Double-check the length of each paper bone by holding it up to its place on the costume. Using the paper patterns, cut 7 bones from beige felt.

**7.** Transfer the Bat Bone pattern on page 85 onto paper (see General Instructions). Pin the paper pattern to each end of each felt strip and trace the shape. Trim both ends of the strip following the shaped tracing.

**8.** At the middle of each felt bone, use the side indentation of the paper pattern to trim a rounded indent into the middle of the bone. This represents a joint in the bone.

**9.** Transfer the Bat Ear pattern on page 85 onto paper (see General Instructions). Using the paper pattern, cut 4 ear pieces from black felt and 2 ear pieces from beige felt. Trim ½" from all edges of the beige ear pieces to create ear insets.

**10.** Fold a large piece of black felt in half and then position the straight edge of the paper wing pattern on the folded edge. Cut through both layers along all scalloped edges.

**11.** With wrong sides facing, glue together the 2 layers of the felt wing. Then, glue on the 5 skeletal bones. Stitch the 2 other skeletal bones to the sleeve fronts of the costume.

**12.** With the bones side of the wings and costume front facing down, stitch or glue the wings to the top edge of the sleeves and along the back of the costume. (The black wings are illustrated in a light shade for contrast.)

**13.** For each ear, you need 1 black front, 1 black back, 1 beige inset, and half the wire. Remember, the ears need to be mirror images of each other (1 right and 1 left), as shown in the photo. On the wrong side of the ear back, mark a line ½" from the outside edge of the ear, everywhere but the short straight edge. Beginning and ending at that short edge, glue the wire along the marked line. Avoid applying glue ½" from the short edge. Trim wire ends even with the fabric.

**14.** Apply glue to the wrong side of each ear front and adhere it to the wrong side (the side with wire) of an ear back. Avoid applying glue ½" from the short edge. Apply glue to the wrong side of each ear inset. With short edges even, adhere 1 inset to each ear front.

**15.** Separate each ear front from its back at the short, unglued edge. Bend 1 wire up to the front and 1 up to the back. To apply the ears to the hood or headband, position them at the center of the hood or band, either horizontally or vertically, and pin them. The inside edges of the 2 ears should touch. Hand stitch or glue the ear seam allowances to the hood or headband. Using a felt-tip pen, draw several curved contour lines on the ear inset, as illustrated.

---

## HOW TO ACT LIKE AN EERIE VAMPIRE BAT

* Bats sleep and hibernate hanging upside down, sometimes from only one leg. Try this on the jungle gym at the playground, but because you do not have wings, be sure to have an adult spot you in case you fall.
* Instead of using their eyes, bats rely on their built-in radar. They scream high-pitched squeaks that bounce off objects and echo back into their big ears to help them judge distances. Practice your own squeaking sounds as you travel from place to place.
* The giant wings of a bat are attached to its arms, legs, and tail. Don't flap your wings—just hold them out straight and soar along the ground by running slowly and quietly.

FOREST FRIENDS

# RASCALLY RABBIT

## How to Paint the Face

**1.** First, using a damp sponge and White #000, cover the entire eye area, including the eyebrows and eyelids and the under-eye area. Then, cover the area above the upper lip, the nostrils, and the chin. Next, using a medium flat brush, create the "teeth," covering the bottom lip at center and three-quarters of the way down the chin.

**2.** Using a damp sponge and Light Gray #122, cover the middle of the forehead with an upside-down triangle between the eyes. Also cover the bridge of the nose and the apples of the cheeks.

**3.** Using a damp sponge and Dark Gray #133, cover the outer areas of the face, including the temples, jawbone, and chin around the "teeth." For contrast, add Black #111 to the sponge and lightly cover the same areas. Blend the black into the dark gray with a clean sponge.

**4.** Using a thin-tip brush and Black #111, outline the "teeth." Paint the tip of the nose, nostrils, and upper lip; connect them at the center with a line. Create a "furry snout" by drawing zigzag lines from the outer nostrils to the corners of the upper mouth. Paint zigzag lines around the eye area. Finally, add "whiskers" to the cheeks and "whisker dots" to the furry snout.

## How to Make the Costume

This costume is made quickly without sewing by adding the chest piece to a sweat suit and making headband-mounted ears. For a softer and warmer rabbit, sew a felt costume body and mount the ears on a sewn hood.

**1.** Purchase a sweat suit or sew a costume body. Also make a ribbon-covered headband or sew a hood. (See General Instructions.)

**2.** Transfer the Rabbit Ear, Rabbit Tail, and Cat Chest patterns on page 85 onto paper (see General Instructions). Using the paper patterns, cut 4 ear pieces from gray felt and 2 ear pieces, 2 tail pieces, and 1 chest piece from white felt. Trim 1" from the 2 long edges of white ear pieces to create ear insets.

**3.** Have the child try on the costume. Then, carefully pin on the chest piece with the wider part at the bottom. Remove the shirt or costume and stitch or glue the chest piece to the costume front.

**4.** To make the tail, pin the 2 tail pieces along the curved edges, and stitch them together. Turn the tail inside out so that the right side is on the outside. Then, stuff it with the polyester stuffing. Pin the tail to the back of the costume below the zipper or to the seat of the sweatpants. Using long hand stitches, attach the tail to the costume.

**5.** For each ear, you need 1 gray front, 1 gray back, 1 white inset, and half the wire. On the wrong side of the ear back, mark a line ½" from the 2 long edges. Beginning and ending at the short straight edge, glue the wire along marked line. Avoid applying glue ½" from the short edge. Trim the wire ends even with the fabric.

**6.** Apply glue to the wrong side of the ear front, then adhere the front to the back with the wrong sides facing. (Avoid applying glue ½" from the short straight edge.) Then, with the short edges even, glue the ear inset to the ear front.

**7.** Separate each ear front from its back at the short, unglued edge. Bend 1 wire up to the front and 1 up to the back.

**8.** To apply the ears to the hood or headband, open the seam allowance and pin them at an equal distance from the center of the hood or band, then glue or stitch them on, leaving 1" to 2" of space between the ears.

## HOW TO ACT LIKE A RASCALLY RABBIT

* Rabbits use their sharp front teeth, called incisors, to bite off grass, fruit, and vegetables (especially farmers' carrots). Then, they use their back teeth, called molars, to grind up the food. Do you know who else has incisors and molars? Ask your dentist.

* Rabbits take many short naps and never sleep soundly. They need to stay alert in case a predator comes near. If danger does appear, they hop away "quick as a bunny" on their strong back legs. Pretend you hear a predator, and hop away as fast as you can.

# SMELLY SKUNK

## How to Paint the Face

**1.** Use a damp sponge and White #000. Begin at the hairline, cover the middle forehead, eyebrows, and eyelids. Paint the nose from the center of the eyebrows to the tip, including the nostrils. Also, paint the area above the lips, extending to a small area on the lower cheek. Cover the center chin.

**2.** Using a damp sponge and Black #111, cover the unpainted areas of the face. Beginning at the hairline, paint the sides of the forehead and temples and continue down around to the tops of the cheeks. Then, cover the outer cheeks and jawbone and under the chin.

**3.** Using a thin-tip flat brush and Black #111, paint the tip of the nose, nostrils, and lips. Paint a line from the center of the nostrils to the upper lip. Create a "furry snout" by drawing zigzag lines from the outer nostrils to the corners of the mouth. Also draw 2 zigzag lines, one on either side of the bottom lip and down to under the chin. For the eyebrows, paint zigzag lines above the child's eyebrows, extending the inner brows straight down to the inner bridge of the nose. Using the brush, add "whisker dots" to the "furry snout".

**4.** Using a medium flat brush and White #111, create whiskers on the cheeks and add zigzag lines under the eyes.

## YOU WILL NEED

* sweat suit or sewn costume body
* sewn hood
* 1 to 1½ yds. of 45"-wide white fur for stripe and tail
* 1 to 1½ yds. of 45"-wide black fur for stripe and tail
* polyester stuffing
* black gloves
* black bumpy chenille stems

## How to Make the Costume

The fastest way to make this costume is to use a hooded sweatshirt. Another good choice is to use a pullover sweatshirt with a sewn hood made from felt. The headband assembly is not suitable for this costume. When shopping, look for fake fur made with long, uncut fur.

**1.** Purchase a sweat suit or sew a costume body. Also sew a hood. (See General Instructions.)

**2.** To measure the torso length, place the tape measure at the top of the child's forehead, measuring over the top of the head, down the back to the hip or to the edge of the sweatshirt.

**3.** To make the torso pattern, draw a rectangle on paper measuring 11" by the measured torso length. To make the torso stripe pattern, draw a rectangle on paper measuring 9" by the measured torso length.

**4.** To measure the tail length, place the tape measure at the child's hip or at the edge of the sweatshirt and allow it to drag 12" on floor.

**5.** To make the tail pattern, draw a rectangle on paper measuring 10" by the measured tail length. To make the tail stripe pattern, draw a rectangle on paper measuring 8" by the measured tail length.

**6.** For all 4 patterns, mark the center of the rectangle at 1 short end. On the torso and torso stripe patterns, draw straight lines from the center mark to the opposite corners. The center triangle is the pattern.

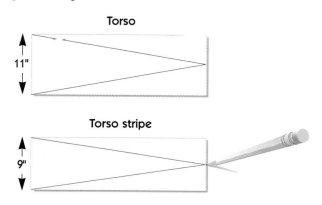

**7.** On the tail and tail stripe patterns, draw curved lines from the center mark to round off 1 end of the rectangle. Cut out the patterns following all inside lines.

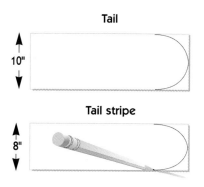

**8.** Using the paper patterns, cut 2 pieces each of the torso and tail from black fur. Cut 2 pieces each of the torso stripe and tail stripe from white fur. Remember, when placing the paper patterns in position on the fur, allow the nap of the fur to stroke smoothly toward the straight end on the torso pieces and the rounded end on the tail pieces.

**9.** With right sides facing and cut edges even, pin and stitch together 2 long edges of the black torso pieces, pivoting at the pointed end. Repeat for the white torso stripe pieces.

**10.** With right sides facing and cut edges even, pin and stitch together the 2 long edges of the black tail pieces, including the curved end. Repeat for the white tail stripe pieces. Trim the seam allowances and turn each section inside out so that the right side is on the outside.

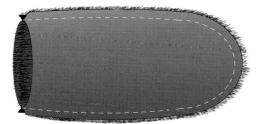

**11.** Fill the black tail loosely with polyester stuffing. With open ends facing, slip the open end of the tail approximately 3" into the open end of the torso. Hand stitch the opening closed.

**12.** With open ends facing, slip the open end of tail stripe into the open end of torso stripe approximately 5". Hand stitch the opening closed.

**13.** Place the white stripe section centered on the black torso/tail section. Hand stitch sections together along all edges.

**14.** Have the child try on the sweatshirt or hooded costume. Pin the fur assembly to the hood and to the back of the sweatshirt, but do not pin it to the sweatpants or below the hip area of the costume. Stitch the fur to the costume along both long edges. If the costume has a zippered opening in the back, stitch the tail assembly along 1 side and safety pin the opposite side to allow easy access to the zipper.

**15.** To make the claws, see step 10 of the Curious Cat on page 4.

## HOW TO ACT LIKE A SMELLY SKUNK

* When frightened, a skunk will lift its tail and spray a terrible odor. The odor is sometimes so strong that it will temporarily stop the "enemy's" breathing, giving the skunk enough time to escape. When wearing your costume, consider wearing too much perfume—it may be as offensive as a skunk's spray.

* Because skunks are nocturnal, their white stripes are easily seen in the dark. When wagged, their tails are like flags, used to warn predators not to come any closer or else…. Practice wagging your tail to help keep predators away.

# WISE OLD OWL

## How to Paint the Face

**1.** Using a damp sponge and Beige Brown #911, cover the face.

**2.** With a wet large flat brush and Metallic Copper #755, create the "owl's eyes." First, outline the eye area. Paint above the eyebrows, down the sides of the nose to the apples of the cheeks and under the eyes. Bring the eyes to points at the temples. Fill in the outlined area.

**3.** Using a large round flat brush and Bright Yellow #222, create the "beak." Outline a diamond shape by making 1 point just below the bridge of the nose (but not between the eyebrows) and the opposite point in the center of the area above the upper lip. Add some spikes above the owl's eyes.

**4.** Using a fine-tip brush and Black #111, outline the beak and paint a line down the center for dimension. Paint a curved line above the eyelids and a thick curved line below the eyes to create "bags." Outline the "owl's eyes" and extend slashes from the outline into the yellow spikes.

**5.** Create feathers by using a thin-tip brush and White #000. Draw rows of scallops across the forehead and chin and below the eyes, staggering them to create feathers. Outline the eyelids and bags under the eyes with tiny slash marks.

## How to Make the Costume

The feathered tunic for this costume can be worn over almost anything. Use a purchased white sweat suit only if you want total coordination of the body and tunic. The owl hood is different from the hood found in the General Instructions. Be careful to trace the right pattern.

**1.** Purchase a sweat suit or sew a costume body. (See General Instructions.)

**2.** To measure child for the winged tunic pattern, see steps 2 through 4 of the Parental Penguin on page 50.

**3.** Using the paper patterns, cut 2 bird tunic pieces and 2 bird wing pieces from beige felt and 2 of each from dark beige felt. Fuse or glue each beige piece to the matching dark beige piece for added weight and body. The dark beige side will be the outside of the costume.

**4.** Choose either the small or large Owl Hood pattern on page 88 and transfer it onto paper (see General Instructions). Using the paper pattern, cut 2 hood pieces from dark beige felt. On 1 hood piece only, cut an opening for the face following the center circle on the pattern.

**5.** With right sides facing and all edges even, pin and stitch the front hood to the back hood along the long curved edge. Turn the hood inside out so that the right side is on the outside.

**6.** To assemble the tunic, see steps 6 through 11 of the Parental Penguin on pages 50–51.

**7.** Separate half of the colored and white feathers for use on the hood and tunic. Measuring approximately 1" from the face opening, stitch or glue the colored feathers to the hood front in a pattern radiating from the center. Stitch or glue the white feathers to the hood over the colored feathers, aligning the ends with the face opening. Repeat with the remaining feathers around the neckline of the tunic.

## HOW TO ACT LIKE A WISE OLD OWL

* Owls have big eyes that help them see easily in the dark. They wait quietly and then swoop down out of the tree to catch rodents for a late night dinner. Be like an owl and quietly sneak up on an unsuspecting family member or friend.

* Screech owls sleep while perched on a tree branch. They wrap their long claws around the branch and lock them in place to sleep. Be a screech owl and see if you can sleep standing up.

* Snowy owls live in cold climates and are completely white, except for a few brown spots. Choose all white feathers and fur for a snowy owl costume.

GENERAL INSTRUCTIONS

## Getting Started: Decisions, Decisions

All of the animal costumes in *Snazaroo Zoo* start with a basic costume body that covers the torso, arms, and legs with one solid color. This look can easily be achieved by purchasing a sweat suit in the appropriate animal color or by sewing a jumpsuit costume using the pattern provided on page 84. It's your choice. You may want to take advantage of all the wonderful materials now available at sewing stores. Felt not only comes in more colors than a crayon box, but it also comes in a variety of textures. Plush and shaggy felt are two new fabrics that make fun, furry animals. And felt is extremely easy to work with! Fake fur is another great costume material. Although a little tricky to work with, it comes in a variety of colors and can be just the thing when a professional, realistic animal is your goal. If sewing isn't your strong suit, or if you want to save time, or if you think your child will feel more comfortable in a sweat suit, you'll choose the sweat suit option. In some cases (such as the Wise Old Owl), a sweat suit is preferred. As you choose the costume you'd like to make, remember that a costume shown with a sewn body can just as easily be created with a sweat suit, and vice versa.

In addition to the costume body type, you'll need to decide what type of head gear to make. You can sew a hood or glue a ribbon covered headband. In most cases, either will support the ears or antennae of the animal. Consider which of these will make the child more comfortable, as well as what the child thinks looks best. Some animals look more realistic with the head fully covered (that is, with a hood) and others (especially the insects) look better with an inconspicuous headband.

The last decision to make is whether the construction of this costume will be a stressful endeavor or a fun family project. Cut, sew, and glue as carefully as possible, but don't be obsessive about it. A little glue showing or an uneven seam is not a disaster. Making a costume should be fun! You'll want something you can be proud of, but chances are the costume will be worn only a few hours. To get the most out of this book, relax and channel your energy into being creative, having a good time, and helping the child wearing the costume to do the same!

## Using the General Instructions

Before making a costume, read through this section (the General Instructions) to learn basic information about creating the costumes and painting the faces. Complete instructions for purchasing a sweat suit, sewing a costume body, sewing a hood, and making the ribbon-wrapped headband are found starting on page 79. This section also includes an easy method for transferring the patterns to paper (page 75), tips on getting a good fit for your costume (pages 75–78), and suggestions for where to purchase supplies (page 74), and much more valuable information.

Once you've reviewed the general instructions, turn to the individual instructions for making the animal costume of your choice. The individual instructions explain how to make the animal's ears, tails, wings, and other "accessories." These features are assembled separately from the costume body and are usually made from felt or fake fur in a coordinating color. When you shop, remember that the yardage and materials listed with the individual animal *do not include materials needed for the costume body and head gear.* You'll need to consult the General Instructions to determine the amounts needed for those.

## Creating Terrific-Looking Faces with Snazaroo Paints

Face painting is great fun and very easy to do if you follow the step-by-step instructions for each animal and use Snazaroo-brand face paints. With a little practice, you'll be creating the perfect tiger stripes or a sassy skunk snout in no time. Snazaroo-brand face paints are FDA-approved (with a "toy safety" rating) and nontoxic. Their vivid colors go on smoothly and dry quickly, enabling you to create multicolored designs with ease. When you're ready to remove Snazaroo paints, just wash them off with soap and warm water or a moistened disposable towelette. If you make any mistakes while creating a face, you can easily wipe them off and start over!

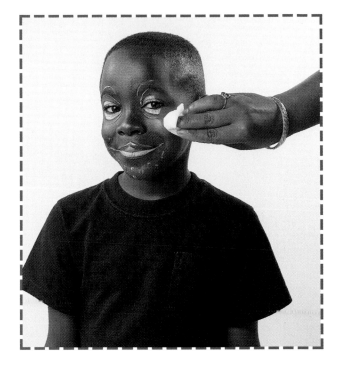

It's a good idea to assemble your paints, sponges, and brushes (all available from Snazaroo) before you start painting a face. Keep some bowls of water (for rinsing brushes, sponges, and washcloths) and some moistened disposable towelettes nearby. Always be extra-careful when working near the eyes. Ask the child to close his or her eyes before applying paint to or wiping paint from this sensitive area. And always stop immediately if the child feels any irritation.

The colors listed for the face paint are Snazaroo color numbers. If you can't find Snazaroo face paints at your local craft store, call 1-800-451-4040. While other brands of face paint can be substituted, be aware that other brands may not be as washable or as safe as Snazaroo paints.

You can paint the child's face before or after he or she has put on the costume, but be sure to protect the costume from the paint. Although the face paint is washable, many parts of the costume are not.

## Ensuring Safety at Snazaroo Zoo

Whether you're assembling or wearing one of the costumes in this book, it's important to act safely and responsibly while having fun it. Keep your project free from injury and disaster by taking the following precautions:

* Do not leave an iron or hot glue gun unattended, and remember to unplug these items when you have finished using them.
* Be careful when using sharp scissors and craft knives, and take care to keep them out of the reach of small children.
* Consider wearing eye protection while at the sewing machine and be sure to keep all hands free of the moving parts. Read and follow the instructions-for-use manual for any additional safety precautions.
* Let children know that they should first ask for an adult's permission before using any tool and that they should proceed only under that adult's supervision.
* Once the costume is complete, trim drawstrings and straps to a reasonable length and, if the costume is flammable, consider treating the costume with a flame-retardant finish.

## Gathering the Basic Supplies

The following is list of general supplies needed for most costumes (in addition to the specific materials listed with each animal). These supplies should be easy to find at your local craft or sewing store.

* sewing machine
* iron and ironing board (when using fusible web adhesive)
* drawing paper (available at art supply stores)
* pencil and air-soluble marking pen
* yardstick, ruler, or tape measure
* chalk
* straight and safety pins
* scissors
* craft knife or wire cutter
* needle and thread
* fusible web
* fabric glue or hot glue and gun
* felt or fake fur (Almost all projects call for one of these. Felt is an easy fabric to cut, sew, and glue and is available in several colors and textures. In addition to the traditional smooth style, felt also comes in a plush or shaggy style. Consider using this nontraditional style for long-haired animals, to give your costume a more realistic look.)

For each individual animal, there is a list of supplies needed. All of those specific supplies can also be found in sewing and craft stores, with the exception of the trash can lid for the turtle shell and the plastic jugs for the elephant and stegosaurus hooves. Look for these at the hardware and grocery stores (the gallon jugs are just empty milk or soda bottles). If you are unfamil-

---

## ENSURING SAFETY—SPECIAL TIPS FOR KIDS

While dressing up in costume is great fun for everyone, it can also be dangerous. Because of wings, tails, and a few extra legs, your overall size while wearing the costume may be greater than what you're accustomed to. To help ensure safety, keep the following tips in mind:

* Step carefully when climbing stairs and walking through doors, especially moving doors and elevators.
* Avoid running or jumping so you don't lose your balance.
* Make sure your vision is not blocked, especially when you put on your head wear.
* Avoid coming close to the kitchen stove, a fireplace, or the open flame of a candle because your costume fabric may be flammable.

 iar with any of the supplies listed, check the glossary on page 89 for a quick definition and, in some cases, information on how to use the supply.

## Transferring Patterns onto Paper

For each of the animal projects in the book, you will create paper patterns to help guide you in cutting the various costume pieces. Some patterns you will create yourself by drawing a circle or rectangle on paper, according to the project's recommended dimensions. Other patterns are provided for you on pages 84–88. Note that the patterns are the correct shapes, but they are too small to use in their printed sizes. To adjust the size to fit your costume, simply draw a larger grid on a larger piece of paper and copy the pattern shape using the boxes as your guide.

**1.** To transfer a pattern to paper, start with a large piece of drawing paper or tape several smaller pieces together. Use gift-wrapping tissue, paper bags, or newspaper if drawing paper is unavailable. You'll also need a yardstick, a felt-tipped marking pen, and a pencil.

**2.** Locate the pattern piece you need to transfer. In straight rows, count the number of grid boxes the pattern covers. Count horizontally at the widest area of the pattern and vertically, at the longest area. Multiply the number of boxes by 3" to determine what size paper to use. Then, using a yardstick and marking pen, draw a grid on your paper with the same number of boxes as the pattern, with each box measuring exactly 3" square. For example, the Cat Ear measures 3 boxes across and 2 boxes down. So, you need paper measuring 9" × 6", and you need to draw a grid showing 3 boxes across and 2 boxes down, each 3" square. *Note:* If you need to transfer several patterns, consider purchasing pattern paper complete with printed grid lines, available at some fabric and art supply stores.

**3.** Using the pencil first, sketch a larger version of the pattern you see in the book following the same angles, curves, and boxes. When you are satisfied with the pattern shape, sharpen the sketched pencil lines with the marking pen and label the pattern by name. Cut out the pattern following the sharpened lines and ignoring the grid.

## Purchasing a Sweat Suit

The fastest assembly for most of the costumes is a hooded sweatshirt and matching sweatpants in the color of the animal. If your sweat suit has a printed logo on the chest, consider wearing it inside out—the fuzzy texture on the wrong side may appear more like animal fur than the right side.

If a sweat suit of the proper color isn't available, any clothing will do, as long as the overall appearance is a one-piece, solid-colored silhouette. If you live in a warm climate or if the costume is for an indoor costume party, use a long-sleeve T-shirt and matching leggings or tights. If you live in a cold climate, consider a lightweight jacket and matching corduroy pants.

*Note:* Because the costume's hood, ears, and tail should all match the color of the sweat suit, bring the suit with you when you shop for felt and supplies to ensure a good match.

## Making the Costume Pattern

The costume body consists of 2 pattern pieces: a jumpsuit and a sleeve. The patterns come in small, medium, and large and are provided on pages 84 and 85. The costume body will fit the average-size child between ages 6 and 12 who is between 3½' and 5½' tall. The costume can be sized up or down to fit someone smaller or taller than this, as explained later in this section. If you're making the costume bigger, remember to buy more fabric.

## Taking Accurate Measurements

Using a flexible tape measure, you'll need to take certain measurements. In the Measurements Needed chart, make a note of each measurement in the first or only blank space provided. Leave the second blank space open at this time.

# MEASUREMENTS NEEDED TO CREATE THE COSTUME

| | CHILD'S MEASUREMENT | INSTRUCTIONS FOR MEASURING CHILD | PATTERN MEASUREMENT | INSTRUCTIONS FOR MEASURING PATTERN |
|---|---|---|---|---|
| CHEST | _____ | Viewing the child from the side, measure his or her fullest part above the waist. Place the tape under the arms and make sure it is parallel with the floor. | | |
| WAIST | _____ | Tie a string comfortably around the middle of the child. Allow the string to roll to the waist. Young children may need to bend to the side to locate the true waistline. Have the child stand straight again and measure at the waist. Do not remove the string yet. | | |
| HIPS | _____ | Measure the fullest part of the child below the waist. Vewing the child from the side will simplify finding the location. | | |
| NECK-TO-WAIST LENGTH | _____ | While viewing the child from behind, ask the child to lower his or her head. Locate the protruding neck bone at the base of the neck and measure from that bone to the waistline string. | _____ | Measure the jumpsuit pattern at the center back/front from the neck edge to the waistline mark on the pattern. The recommended cutting length should be 4" to 6" longer than the child's measurement. |
| PANTS LENGTH | _____ | Measure the child along the side of the leg from the waistline string to a few inches from the floor, where hemmed pants would end. | _____ | Measure the jumpsuit pattern from the waistline mark to the bottom edge of the costume. The recommended cutting length should be 3" to 5" longer than the child's measurement. |
| SLEEVE LENGTH | _____ | Locate the base of the neck at the side by having the child tilt his or her head sideways. With the child's head upright again, have the child put a hand on his or her hip. Measure from the base of the neck, over the bent elbow to the wrist bone. | _____ | Measure the sleeve pattern from the neckline to the bottom edge of the sleeve. The recommended cutting length should be 2" to 3" longer than the child's measurement |

## TIPS FOR ASSEMBLING THE COSTUME AND ACCESSORIES

* To make the best use of the fabric and prevent mistakes, pin and cut the costume body, hood, and "accessory pieces" at the same time. While plain felt shows no discernible difference between the right and wrong side of the fabric, fake fur and plush or shaggy felt do have a right and wrong side. For these fabrics, pay attention to how the pieces are cut and assembled to ensure the right sides wind up on the outside of your costume. When you cut 2 or more pieces from the same pattern, fold the fabric in half lengthwise with the right sides facing and cut the 2 pieces at once. This will guarantee a mirror image of each piece, to ensure a right and left to the costume body or right and left ears. For long-haired fur, stroke the fabric with your hand to determine which direction you would like the nap to run. To prevent uneven shading or fur from "growing" in 2 different directions, position all the pattern pieces with the nap running in the same direction—usually down on the body.

* Before sewing the pieces together at the seam, pin fabrics together with right sides facing unless otherwise noted. All pattern pieces include a ½" seam allowance. Stitch pieces together using a medium-length straight stitch. Trim all seams to ¼" after sewing.

* To adhere pieces together, choose fabric glue, hot glue, or fusible web. Because of its quick drying time, hot glue is the fastest method. Fabric glue, on the other hand, is the easiest method to use, and fusible web avoids glue bleed-through. Generally, the glues are used to adhere small intricate areas like seam allowances, and fusible web is used on large, flat areas. The individual instructions usually recommend the best method for the particular step, but don't hesitate to change to the adhesive method you prefer.

### Determining Pattern Size

Review your noted chest, waist and hip measurements to determine which size pattern to use. Transfer the jumpsuit and sleeve pattern to several large pieces of paper measuring 30" × 40". Refer to page 75 to learn how to transfer patterns to paper.

### PATTERN SIZES

|          | CHEST   | WAIST   | HIP     |
|----------|---------|---------|---------|
| SMALL    | 21"–24" | 20"–22" | 22"–25" |
| MEDIUM   | 24"–27" | 22"–24" | 25"–28" |
| LARGE    | 27"–30" | 24"–26" | 28"–32" |

### Making Length Adjustments

Children grow at different rates, causing some kids with similar chest and hip measurements to have dramatically different leg, sleeve, and back measurements. To determine if the length of the pattern needs to be adjusted, you'll need to measure the paper pattern. First, fill in the "Pattern Measurement" column of the Measurements Needed chart on page 77 by using a tape measure or a yardstick and following the instructions in the last column of the chart. Keep in mind that for all measurements, the recommended cutting lengths for the pattern are greater than the child's measurements. These additional inches are needed for comfort in sitting, walking, and stretching, as well as for hems and elastic casings.

Compare the child's measurements to the actual pattern measurements. If the pattern lengths need to be adjusted to meet the recommended cutting lengths, simply mark the paper pattern with a horizontal line at a point midway in the measurement. Add or subtract the necessary number of inches by adding a strip of paper or folding the pattern. Draw lines to even-up both side edges of the pattern through the fold or the extension.

To shorten
waist length

To
lengthen
sleeve
length

To lengthen
pant length

# Sewing the Costume Body

## YOU WILL NEED

* felt or fake fur
* zipper or ½" wide Velcro, 18" long
* ⅞ yd. of ½" wide single-fold bias tape
* 2 yds. of ⅜" wide elastic

Use the Costume Yardage Chart to determine the number of yards of felt or fur needed for the costume body. If you are making a matching hood, add ½ yard to the yardage listed in the 36"-wide fabric column. The yardage listed in the 72"-wide fabric column provides enough extra fabric to cut a hood. Also, add or subtract the appropriate number of inches if length alterations were made to the jumpsuit or sleeve pattern. Yardage for the "accessory pieces" is not included.

## COSTUME YARDAGE CHART

| | 36" wide fabric | 72"-wide fabric |
|---|---|---|
| SMALL | 4 yds. | 2 yds. |
| MEDIUM | 3¾ yds. | 2¼ yds. |
| LARGE | 4¾ yds. | 2½ yds. |

**1.** Transfer the jumpsuit and sleeve patterns on pages 84 and 85 in the appropriate size onto paper. Piece and tape together the upper and lower jumpsuit patterns at the break. Cut 4 jumpsuit pieces and 2 sleeve pieces from felt in the appropriate animal color.

**2.** With all edges even, pin and stitch together 2 jumpsuit pieces along the center front edge from neck edge to curved crotch. Set aside.

**3.** The zipper or Velcro strip is inserted into the back neck as follows. First, pin together the 2 remaining jumpsuit pieces along the center back edge. With the top edges even, place the zipper or Velcro in position on the seam. Using chalk, mark the fabric at the bottom zipper stop or lower edge of the Velcro. Remove the zipper or Velcro.

**4.** To apply the zipper, stitch a ½"-wide seam in the center back, setting the machine to a basting stitch above the chalk mark and a regular stitch length below the chalk mark. Press the seam open. With the right side of the zipper facing the pressed-open seam, pin and hand baste the zipper in place on the wrong side of the costume. Stitch both sides and the bottom edge of the zipper through all layers. Remove the hand basting stitches.

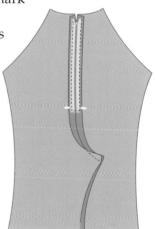

**5.** To apply the Velcro, stitch a ½"-wide seam from the chalk mark to the lower edge of the crotch. Above the chalk mark, turn the fabric under ½" and hand baste the seam allowance in place on half of the seam only. Leave the other half of the seam unfolded. Separate the Velcro halves. Work with the soft half of the Velcro and the basted seam first. With the fold of the fabric even with 1 long edge of the Velcro, pin the Velcro to the costume back, covering the seam

allowance. Stitch all edges of the Velcro through both layers of fabric. Work with the rough half of the Velcro and the extended seam next. With 1 long edge of the Velcro even with the fabric edge, pin the Velcro to the costume back on the extended seam. *Note:* If the Velcro is wider than the seam allowance, allow the Velcro to extend past the cut edge of the fabric. Stitch on all edges of the Velcro through the single layer of fabric.

**6.** With right sides together, even up the neck edges and match the curved sleeve seams, then pin and stitch 1 sleeve to the jumpsuit front. Repeat for the remaining sleeve. In the same manner, pin and stitch the remaining curved sleeve seams to the jumpsuit back.

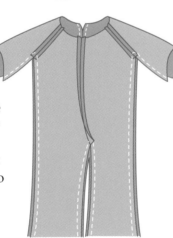

**7.** With all edges even and right sides together, pin the back assembly to the front. Stitch together the sleeve underarm seams and side front and back seams. Also stitch together the inner leg seams.

**8.** On each sleeve and pants edge, turn under and press ¾". Pin into place. Beginning near a seam, stitch through both layers ½" from the folded edge leaving a small 2" break in the stitches. Cut 2 pieces of elastic, each 3" longer than the child's wrist measurement and 2 pieces, each 3" longer than the child's ankle measurement. Using a safety

pin, insert elastic into and back out of the casing tunnel through the break in the stitches.

**9.** Overlap ends of the elastic by 1". Pin then stitch together the ends of the elastic. Allow the elastic to draw back and be hidden in the casing. Stitch the felt to connect the break in the stitches, closing up the casing opening. Avoid stitching through the hidden elastic.

**10.** Cut a piece of bias tape approximately 3" longer than the neck opening of the costume. Open out 1 fold of the bias tape and press lightly. With the right sides facing and the cut edges even, pin the bias tape to the neck edge of the costume. On both ends allow ½" of tape to extend past the center back seam of the costume—trim the tape ends if necessary. Fold back the ½" extensions and pin aligning folded edges even with folded edge of seam.

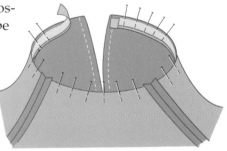

**11.** Stitch the tape to the costume, placing the needle in the opened-out crease of the tape. This seam allowance will measure approximately ¼". Turn the tape to the wrong side of the costume and press. Pin and stitch the tape in place along the outer fold using hand or machine stitches.

# Sewing the Costume Hood

Whether you chose to make your costume body from felt, fur, or a sweat suit, a sewn hood in a matching color may be just the head wear that is needed to support ears or a head dress. A hood is appropriate for most costumes except the bugs and bees that wear antennae and the owl that has a hood pattern of his own. In general, children 4 ½' or less will fit into the small hood and those taller than 4 ½' will need the large hood. You can alter the size slightly by stitching a wider or narrower seam allowance.

## YOU WILL NEED

* ½ yd. of felt or fake fur or scraps reserved from costume body
* ¾ yd. of single-fold bias tape
* 1¼ yds. of ⅛"-wide cording
* 2 pieces of Velcro dots or squares

**1.** Transfer the Hood pattern on page 84 in the appropriate size onto paper. Cut 2 hood pieces from felt in the appropriate animal color.

**2.** With all edges even and right sides facing, pin and stitch together 2 hood pieces along the long outside curved edge. Turn hood right side out.

**3.** Open out 1 fold of the bias tape and press. With the right sides facing and the cut edges even, pin the bias tape to the long inside curved edge, begin pinning at the short straight edge of

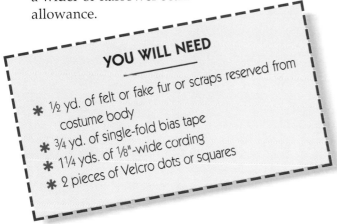

the hood, continue over the seam and end at the opposite short straight edge. Stitch the tape to the hood, placing the needle in the opened-out crease of the tape. This seam allowance will measure approximately ¼". Wrap the tape to the wrong side of the hood and pin. Along the edge of the inside fold, stitch tape to the hood, creating a casing.

**4.** On right side of the hood, along the casing edge, measure and mark ¾" from each short straight edge. Cut a slit in the felt of the casing. Do not cut the bias tape below. On 1 edge only, turn under ¾" and press.

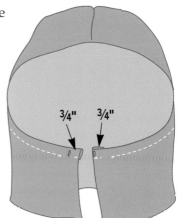

**5.** Pin and stitch 2 rough Velcro halves through 2 layers of felt on the inside of the folded side of the hood, and 2 soft halves through a single layer of felt on the inside of the other side of the hood.

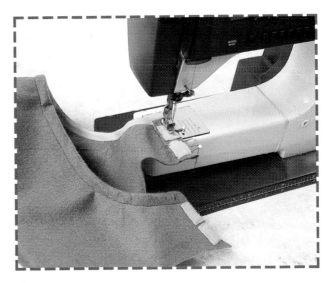

**6.** Pin a safety pin to 1 end of the cord. Using the pin as a guide, pull the drawstring through the casing, entering and exiting through slits in the casing. Remove the safety pin and knot both ends of the cord.

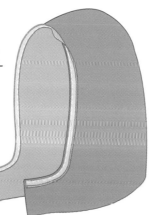

# Ribbon-Covered Headband for Antennae or Ears

Ribbon-covered headbands provide a good, nonslip base for mounting ears or antennae. When mounting antennae, tuck the pompon-topped stems under the ribbon as you wind it around the band. Once the band is wrapped, the Beautiful Butterfly is created by gluing the 2 pompons together. For the Busy Bumblebee, wrap each stem around a fat pencil to create a coil. Those materials and steps marked with a ✱ are for antennae headbands only.

## YOU WILL NEED

✱ plastic headband
✱ 1½ yds. of ⅝"-wide ribbon or a felt strip of equal dimensions
✱✱ 2 chenille stems, 12" long
✱✱ 2 acrylic pompons, 1½" wide

**✱1.** On each chenille stem, glue 1 pompon to 1 end and bend a 1" 90-degree angle on the opposite end. On outside center of the headband, measure and mark 2 antennae positions 1½" apart and equidistant from the center of the band.

**2.** On 1 end of the ribbon, cut off 1 corner at a 45-degree angle. Beginning at 1 inside end of the headband, position the cut edge of the ribbon even with 1 side edge of the headband and glue. For the first few inches, wrap the ribbon around the headband at an angle slightly overlapping last layer.

**✱3.** As you approach the first mark, stop and glue the ribbon to the headband. Apply glue to the bent extension of 1 stem and adhere it to the headband at the mark. Wrap the ribbon on both sides of the stem covering the extension. Repeat for the remaining stem and remaining mark.

**4.** Continue wrapping and pulling the ribbon taught until you reach the opposite end. Secure the end with glue.

## ACTING LIKE YOUR FAVORITE ANIMAL

✱ Once your costume is completed and you look like your favorite Snazaroo Zoo animal, review the section that tells you how to act the real thing. Whether you're growling, clawing, or flapping your wings, the most important thing you can do is use your imagination. Consider what you already know about your animal—and then read up to find out even more. Uncover the animal's most endearing qualities and learn to mimic them. For fun, you can even carry a prop representing the animal's favorite food or habitat.

✱ Many of the animals in Snazaroo Zoo enjoy each others company. Try teaming up with some of your friends and be animal buddies. Be a tortoise and a hare, a cat and a dog, a litter of rabbits with your brothers and sisters, or a wild animal safari with your scout troop friends.

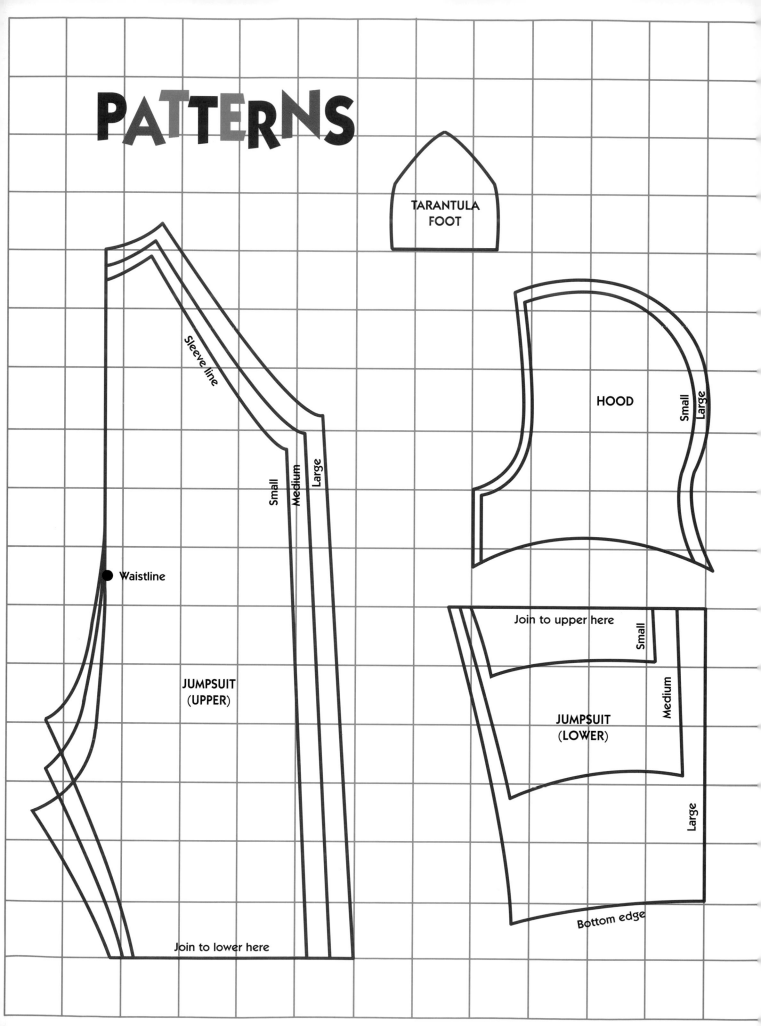

# PATTERNS

**TARANTULA FOOT**

Sleeve line

Waistline

Small
Medium
Large

JUMPSUIT
(UPPER)

Join to lower here

HOOD

Small
Large

Join to upper here

Small

Medium

JUMPSUIT
(LOWER)

Large

Bottom edge

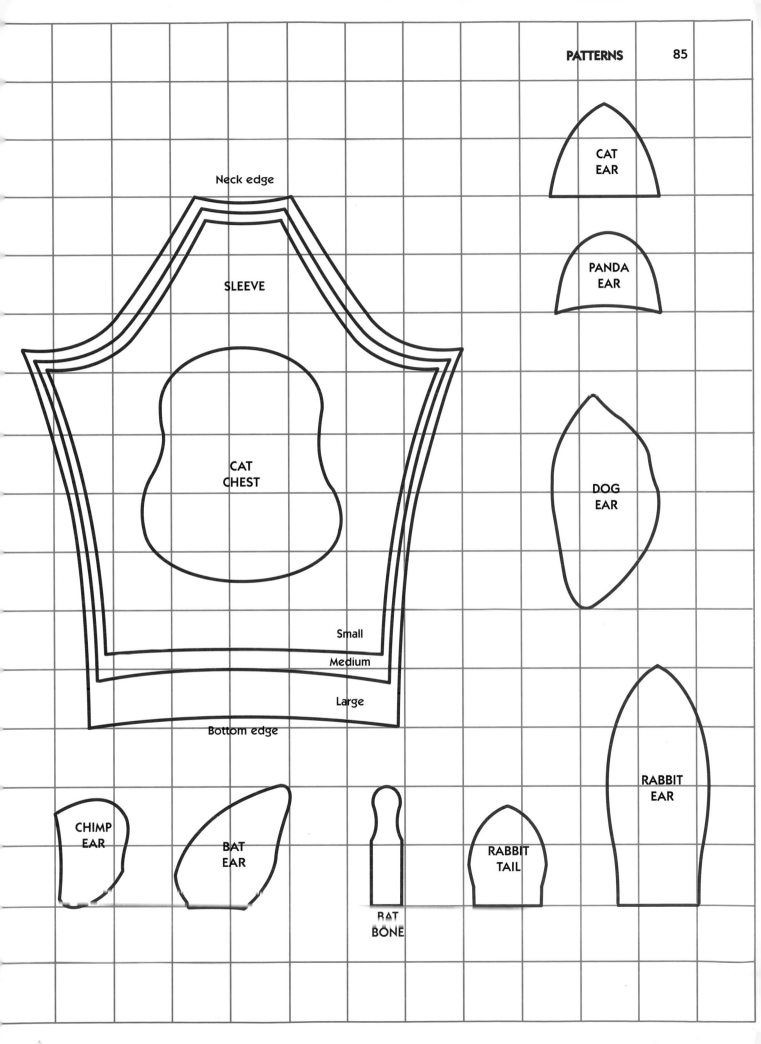

CAT EAR

PANDA EAR

DOG EAR

Neck edge

SLEEVE

CAT CHEST

Small

Medium

Large

Bottom edge

RABBIT EAR

CHIMP EAR

BAT EAR

RAT BONE

RABBIT TAIL

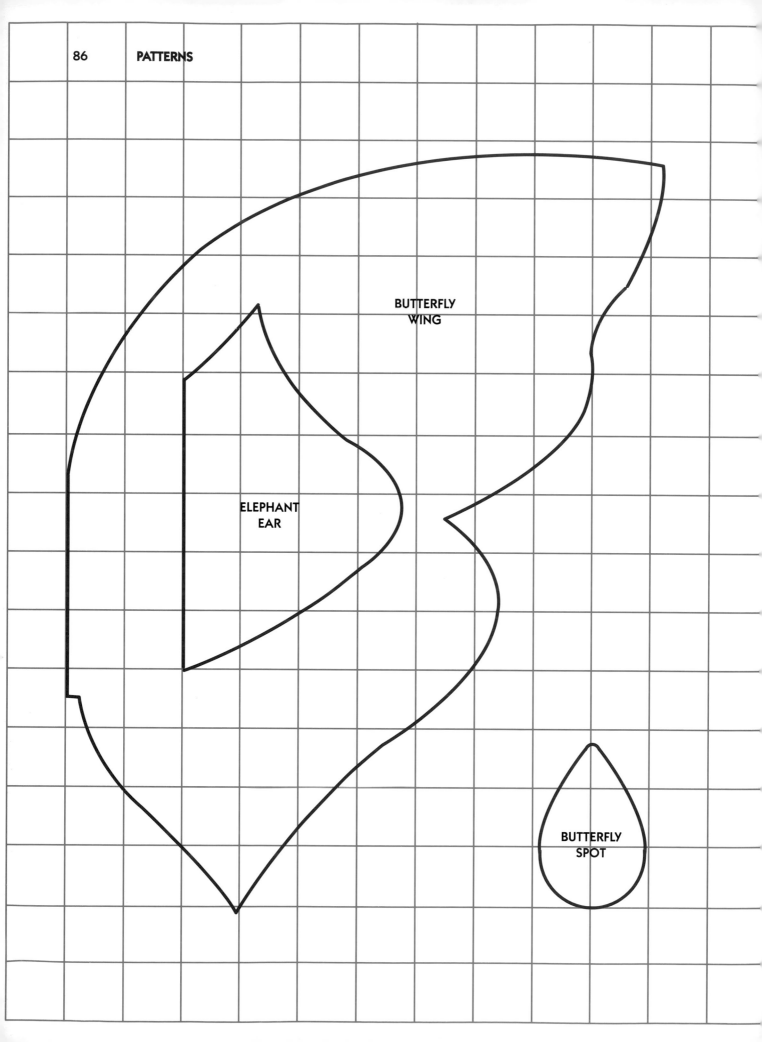

BUTTERFLY
WING

ELEPHANT
EAR

BUTTERFLY
SPOT

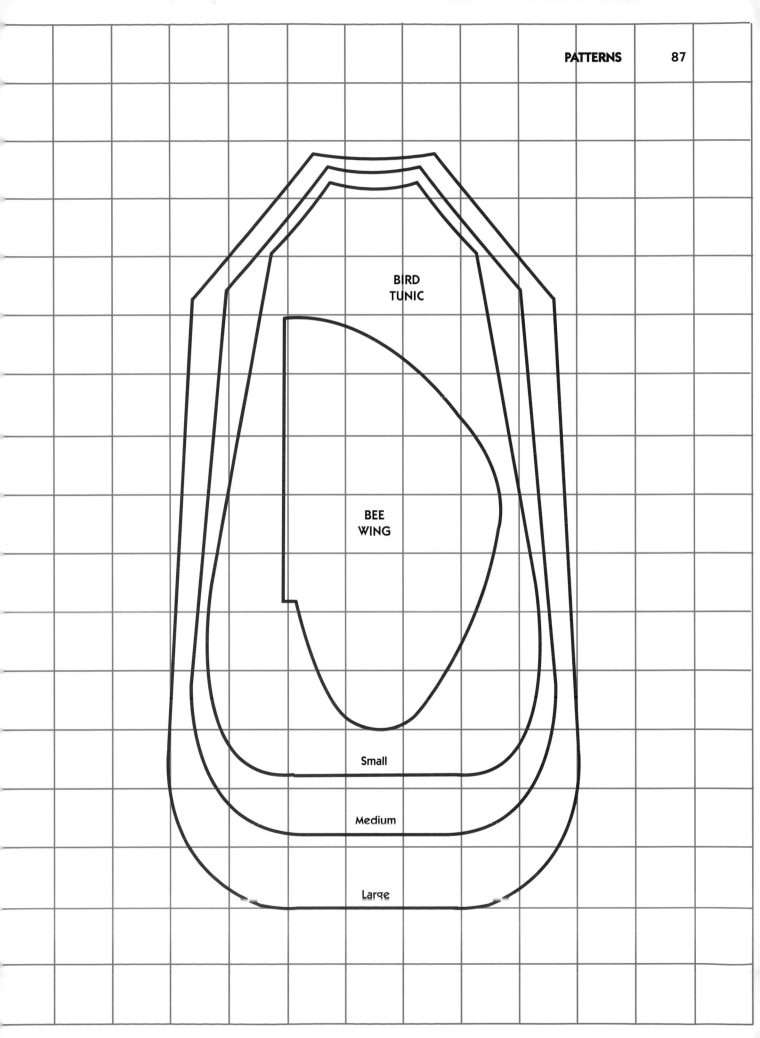

BIRD
TUNIC

BEE
WING

Small

Medium

Large

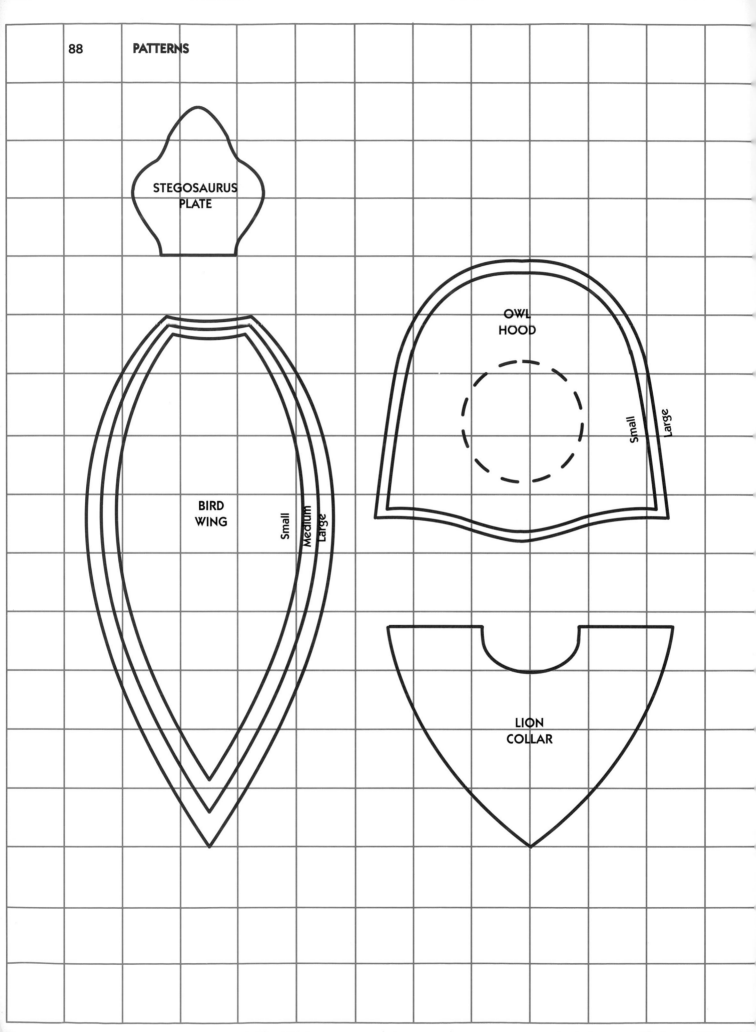

STEGOSAURUS
PLATE

BIRD
WING

Small
Medium
Large

OWL
HOOD

Small

Large

LION
COLLAR

**AIR-SOLUBLE MARKING PEN.** Felt-tip pen designed to mark fabric temporarily until permanent stitching or gluing can be accomplished. Water-soluble pens work similarly, but their marks must be rinsed out with water.

**BASTE.** To stitch temporarily by hand or machine using a long, loose stitch that can be easily removed once the permanent stitching or gluing has been accomplished.

**BLEND.** Eliminating a distinct edge along a face-painted area by rubbing the paint gently into the adjoining colored area.

**BUMPY CHENILLE STEM.** *See Chenille Stem.*

**CASING.** A fabric tunnel in which elastic or cord can be inserted to adjust the fullness of a garment. Casings are created by double-folding an edge of the garment or by attaching a piece of bias tape to the garment.

**CHENILLE STEM.** A yarn-covered wire similar to a pipe cleaner. The yarn on bumpy chenille stems varies in thickness every few inches.

**CORDING.** A decorative string or rope designed to be used as a drawstring in clothing.

**CRAFT KNIFE.** A pencil-shaped tool with a replaceable blade designed to make sharp cuts in paper, plastic, and other craft materials.

**D RINGS.** Metal buckle-type fasteners shaped like the letter *D* that are used in pairs with flexible belting woven between them.

**FLEXIBLE WINDOW RODS.** Contemporary curtain rods designed to mount at the base of half-circle windows by attaching at each end and being flexible enough to curve outward.

**FOAM RUBBER.** Soft rubber fiber with air bubbles incorporated into its structure, giving it a springlike resistance. It is available in cut pieces or by the yard in several densities and thicknesses.

**FUSIBLE WEB.** A fabric adhesive that is a loosely woven mesh fabric often backed with paper. It adheres two layers of fabric when inserted between them and pressed. The paper backing allows the fabric layers to be pressed one at a time, which makes positioning and smoothing the fabrics easier.

**HAND STITCH.** Any method of stitching two or more fabric layers together using a hand sewing needle and thread.

**HOT GLUE GUN.** An electric "gun-shaped" tool that melts companion sticks of glue in its inner chamber and dispenses the melted glue when its "trigger" is pulled.

**NAP.** A fabric finish created during construction by brushing the fabric yarns to produce a directional, fuzzy texture on one side. The yarns often rise at an angle.

**POLYESTER STUFFING.** A soft, springy, fibrous material used as padding or filling in fabric projects.

**QUILT BATTING.** Traditionally, a thick insulating fabric used between two layers of fabric to add warmth and thickness. Batting is now available in a variety of materials and thicknesses.

**SANDWICH BOARD.** Traditionally, two sign boards connected along the top edge and designed to be worn over the shoulders. This concept is adapted for several of the costumes using felt-covered poster board taped together at the shoulders.

**SEAM.** A line of stitching that attaches two layers of fabric and is usually placed ½" from the outside edge of the aligned fabrics.

**SEAM ALLOWANCE.** The area of layered fabric between a stitched seam and the outside edge of the fabrics.

**SINGLE-FOLD BIAS TAPE.** A prefolded strip of lightweight fabric cut on the bias grain for flexibility that usually measures approximately ½" folded (both edges are folded and meet at the center on the backside of the tape). Bias tape is used to enclose cut edges and as an enclosure for elastic; it is sold in packages or by the yard.

**VELCRO.** A brand of nylon fastener that follows the same principle as a hook and eye. One side is covered with small nylon hooks, the opposite side with small nylon "eyes." When pressed together, the two sides hold tight until pulled apart. Also called hook-and-loop fastener, it is available in varying widths and strengths and sold by the yard or packaged as strips, dots, or squares.